D0427122

more brain-boosters

by David Webster

with photographs by the author

Doubleday & Company, Inc.
Garden City, New York

ISBN: 0-385-02091-0 Trade
0-385-02497-5 Prebound
Library of Congress Catalog Card Number 73-78092

Printed in the United States of America
First Edition

contents

photo credits

p. 93, 94 (top) Courtesy of
The American Museum of Natural History
p. 87, 90 (top) Steven Cochran
p. 16 (top), 43, 95 (bottom) George Cope
p. 21 (left), 41 (top and middle), 45, 48
Educational Development Center
p. 91 (top) Jeff Haase
p. 1 (bottom), 44 (top left and top right),
50, 53, 94 (bottom), 95 (top),
100 (top and bottom), 102 Joan Hamblin
p. 11 (top) Madison Judson
p. 44 (bottom) Franklyn D. Lauden
p. 11 (bottom) Roy Mittelhan
p. 9 Major Morris
p. 8 NASA
P. 15 (top and bottom) Victor Stokes
p. 64 (top) Triborough Bridge
and Tunnel Authority

All other photos by the author

more brain-boosters

1 shadows

How do you hold a stick in the sun so that it seems to cast no shadow?

The shadow of one matchbox was made by sunlight. The other shadow was made in the light from an electric bulb. Can you tell which is which?

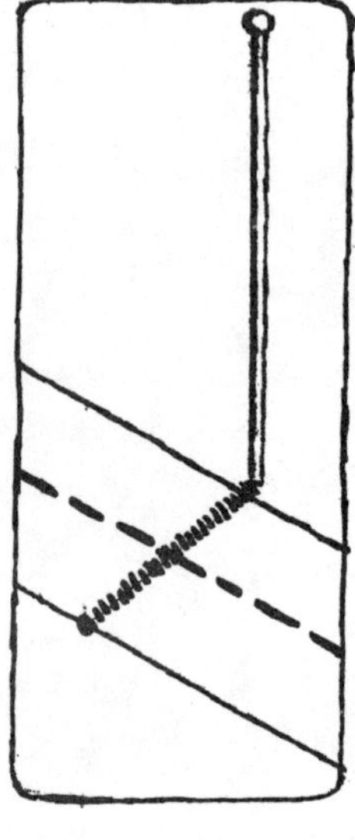

Suppose there was a flagpole that cast a shadow like this at 10:00 A.M. on the morning of April 14.

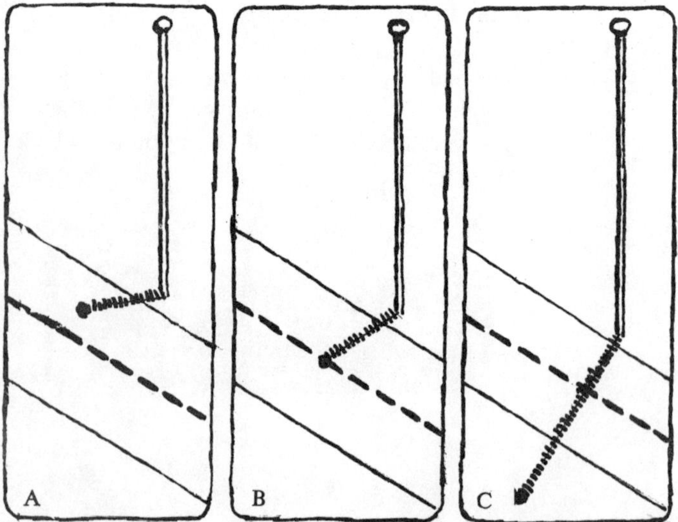

How would the pole's shadow look at other times and on different days? Match the sketches with each of these times:

Noon on April 14?
10:00 A.M. on June 14?
10:00 A.M. on October 14?

Finding north with the sun's shadow

Here is one way to find north without a compass. At about 11:00 A.M. on a sunny day, push a pencil into the ground so its sticks up straight. Scratch a circle around the pencil, using the length of the shadow as the radius. Then with a pebble mark the spot where the shadow touches the circle. The shadow will continue to move and to grow shorter as noon approaches. Check occasionally until the shadow again touches the circle in a different place at some time after twelve noon. Mark the new spot with another pebble, and scratch a line between the two pebbles. Draw another line from the middle of the first line toward the stick. This line points to true north and south.

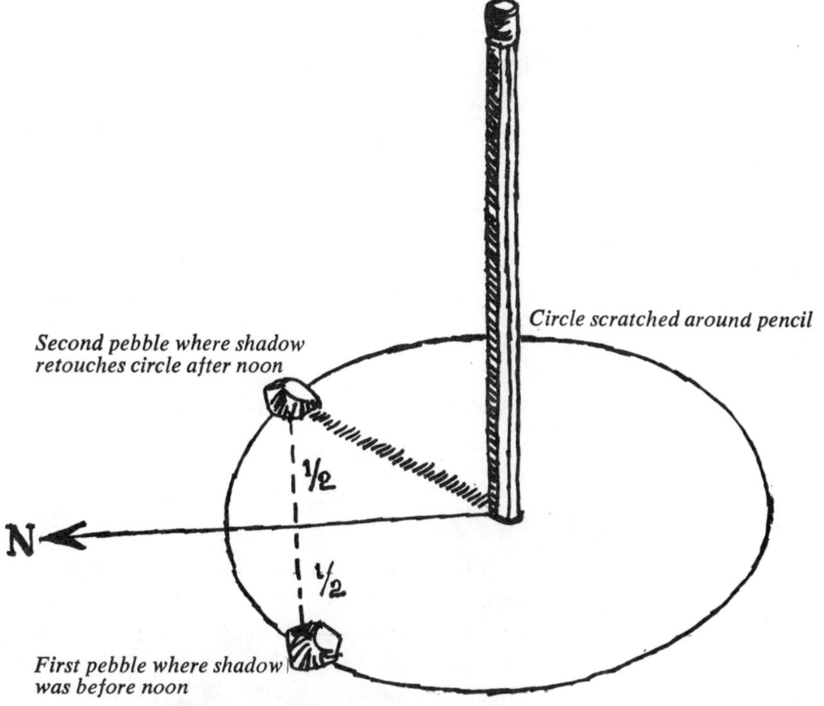

Figure out from the shadows whether this noontime picture was taken in New Jersey or in California.

For science experts only

. . . Is the sun's shadow always shortest at noon?

. . . Does a soap bubble cast a shadow?

. . . Can a shadow ever be smaller than the object that makes it?

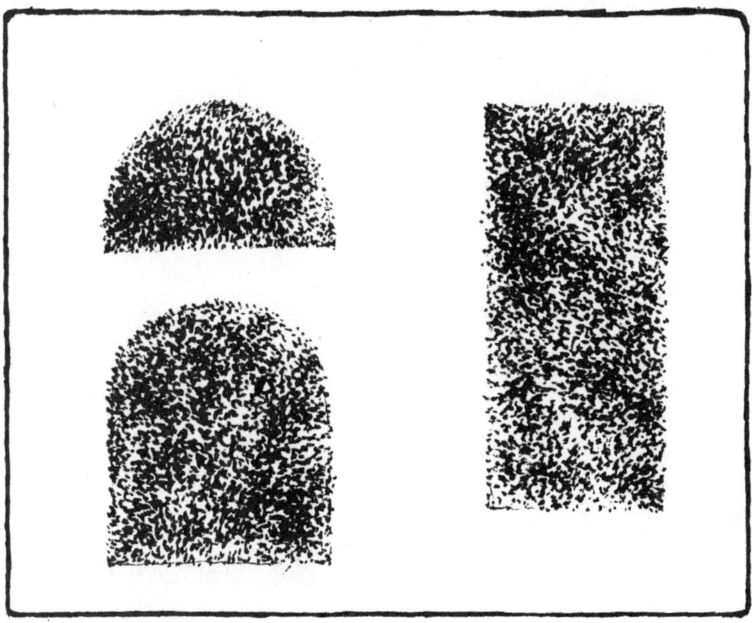

Can you do it?

The three drawings show shadows made by an object held in different positions in front of a light. How can you make something that would cast the same shadows?

How can you make a square shadow with an unfolded postcard?
How can you make a round spot of light with a tiny square hole?
How can you hold a pencil so it makes two shadows?

6
Mystery photos

What made these shadows?

Shadows on the moon

Why are the moon's craters easiest to see along the bottom edge?
Where is the sun?
How much of the moon is in darkness?

2 mystery photos

Explain the unusual patterns on the wall.

10

Which way is up?

11

12

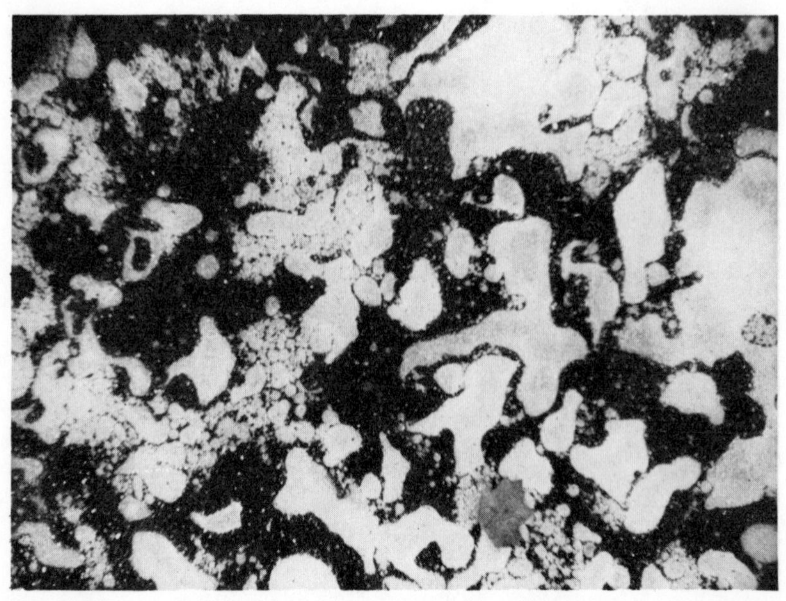

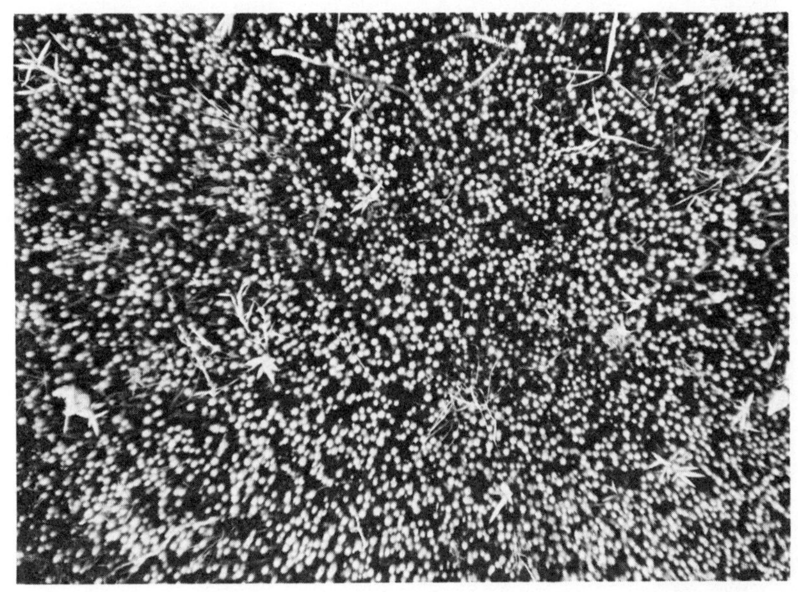

One is green, and one is old;
One is brown, and one is cold.

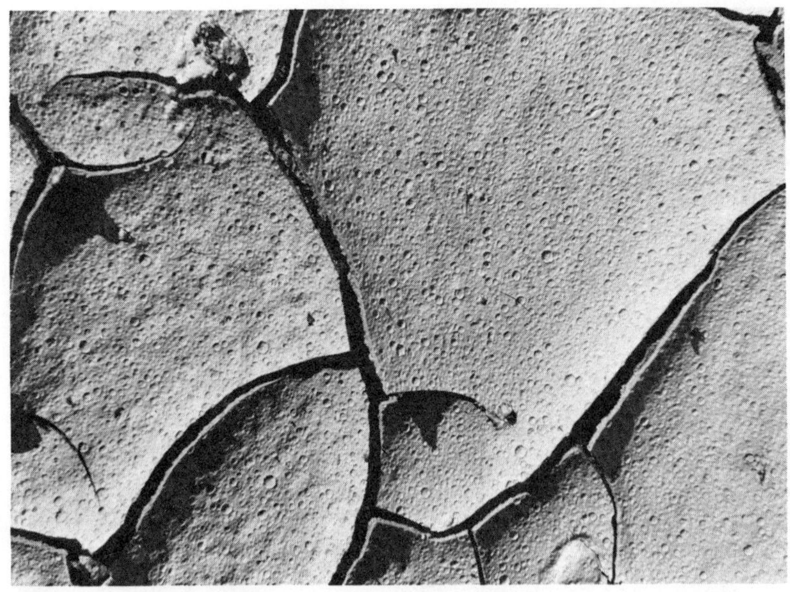

What are these?

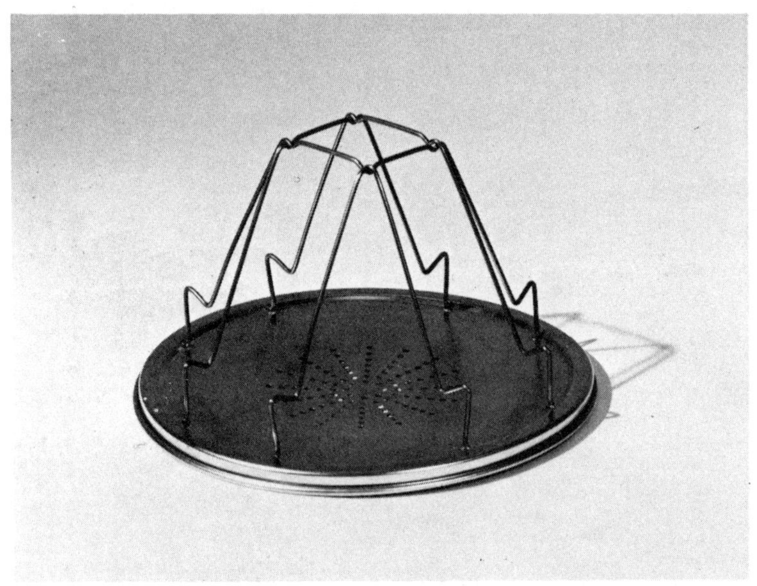

Your grandmother may have used this in the kitchen.

These are sold in sport stores.

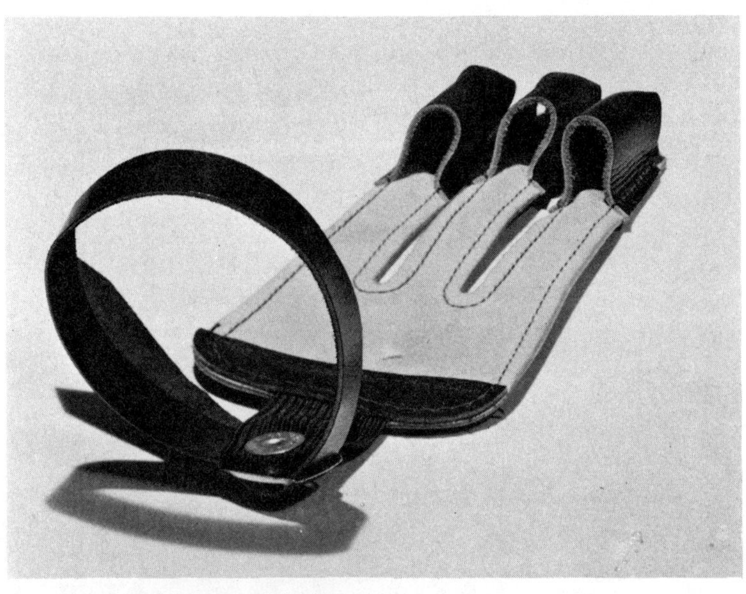

Most paper wasp nests are round, but this one is square. Where might the wasps have made it?

How can sea gulls stand on water?

Notice how miniature sand dunes have formed over the small bushes. Was the wind blowing from the left or the right?

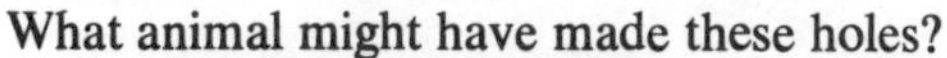

What animal might have made these holes?

Why are the letters so much wider in some parts than in others?

What causes white lines like these to form near melting piles of snow along the road?

3 drops and bubbles

Making drops

. . . Take a glass of water outdoors and throw the water up into the air. You should see that some of the water forms drops. Are all the drops the same size?

. . . Watch water drip from a faucet. What happens to the drops as you slowly open the faucet to let out more water?

. . . Heat a frying pan on the stove and sprinkle water into it. What causes the drops to roll around in the hot pan?

. . . Get a small glass of cooking oil and place a drop of water on top. If it floats, push the drop down into the oil with your finger. What shape does the drop take as it slowly falls through the oil?

. . . Fill a round balloon with water and place it on the table. Water drops and water balloons are alike in several ways.

. . . Sleet is frozen water drops. If you drip melted sealing wax into water it will harden into little balls. Can you guess how lead shot is made?

20
Experiment with drops

Wet your hand and sprinkle some water onto a piece of wax paper. Are all of the drops the same size and shape?

Look at different-sized drops from the side. What is wrong with this drawing of water drops?

You can move your drops around with a pencil point. What do you think makes the drop stretch out and cling to the pencil?
Push two or three small drops together to make a bigger drop. Then take two pencils and try to pull the bigger drop apart to make two smaller ones. Can you make a water drop smaller than a pinhead?
Touch a drop with a piece of soap. What happens to the drop's shape?
Place the wax paper on a printed page. Look at the letters through the drops. Do large drops magnify more than smaller ones?
Now tip the paper slowly, and watch the drops begin to roll down. Do the small drops roll before the larger ones?
Make drops with different liquids, such as alcohol, kerosene, and oil. Can you identify an unknown drop by examining its shape?

Mystery photos

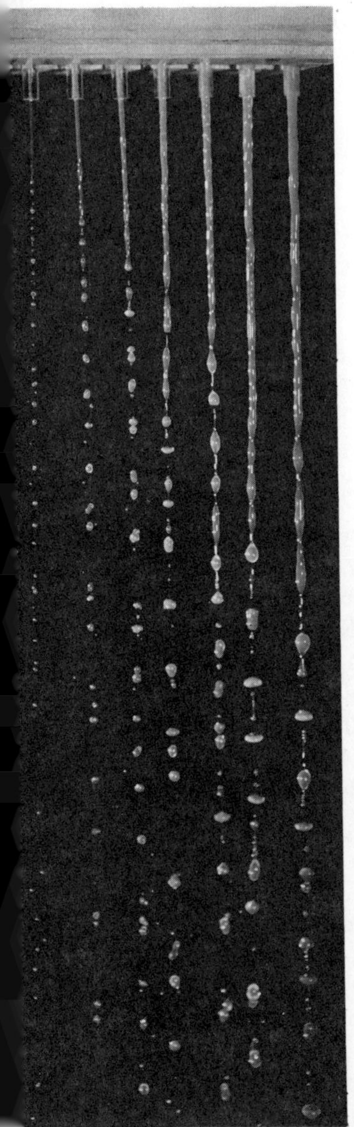

Why do the streams of water break up into drops at different places?

What caused these drops?

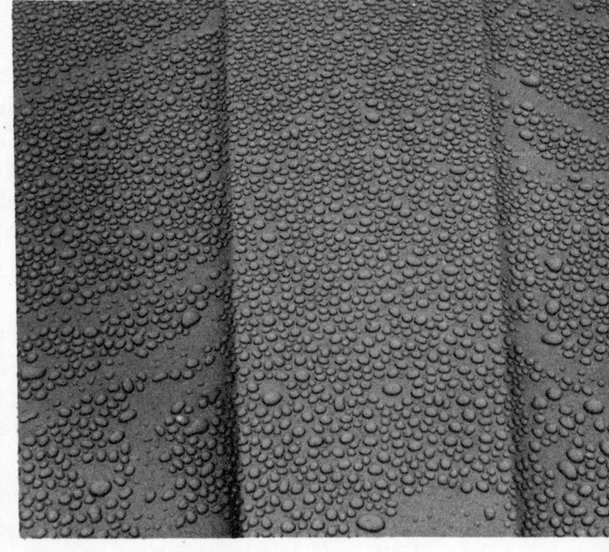

How much water is there in a drop?

Use an eyedropper or straw to drip water into a teaspoon until it is full. Then see how many teaspoons of water there are in an 8-ounce measuring cup. Which of these answers is closest to the weight of a water drop: 1/10th of an ounce, 1/100th of an ounce, 1/400th of an ounce?

For science experts only

. . . Why are drops always roundish and never square?
. . . What is the largest hardened drop you have ever seen?
. . . What is the difference between a drop and a bubble?

Air drops

Blow through a straw into the bottom of a glass of water. Can you see any gas bubbles?
You can watch bubbles better in a jar of thick liquid like cooking oil or Karo syrup. Turn a full jar upside down so the small air space is on the bottom. What shape is the bubble as it rises? Then shake up a partly filled bottle to mix the air with the syrup. Which bubbles rise faster? Do all the drops eventually float to the surface?

Soap bubbles

Mix up a soap bubble solution with two caps of dishwashing liquid in a glass of cold water. There are many types of wands you can use to blow bubbles. An old pipe, a wire loop, or a small funnel work well. If you try a straw, split and fold back the end. Wire screening of different sizes can also be used.

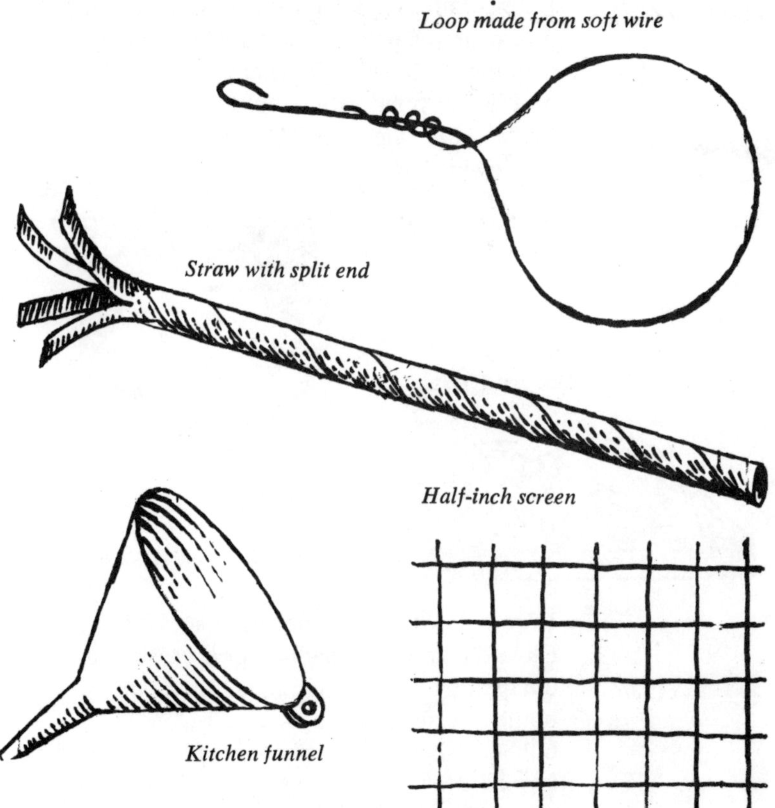

Dip the wand into the bubble solution, lift it out, and blow gently on the soap film or wave it through the air. You will have to pour the bubble solution into a shallow tray in order to wet the larger wands.

If you have trouble making large bubbles or bubbles that last a long time, try changing your bubble solution. Perhaps you should add more soap. Some bubble blowers say that adding a teaspoon of sugar or glycerine helps make better bubbles. Also, rain water might be used instead of tap water, which could contain minerals. You will have to experiment yourself to find what works best.

Bubble rafts can be made by blowing through a straw into a pan of soap bubble solution. Continue to blow until the entire surface becomes covered with bubbles. Are all the bubbles the same size? Can you vary their size by blowing harder or softer, or by using a larger straw?

Here is how to make bubbles float in "mid-air." Close the drain in a bathtub or large sink, and dump in a box of baking soda. Then pour in a bottle of vinegar and add some water. The bubbling shows that carbon dioxide gas is being formed. Now blow soap bubbles and let them drop into the sink. The bubbles should float on the layer of carbon dioxide until they break.

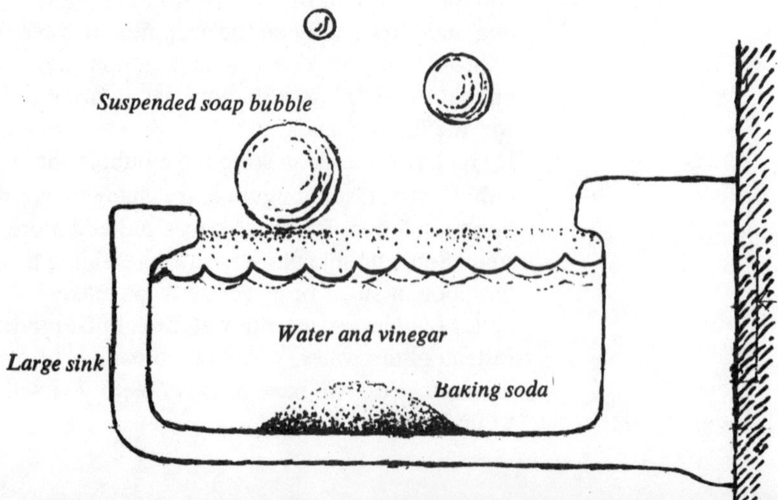

Can you do it?

. . . can you freeze a soap bubble outside on a very cold day?

. . . can you blow one soap bubble inside of soap bubble?

. . . can you blow one soap bubble inside of another soap bubble?

4 balloons

Can you do it?

. . . can you hold a balloon filled with air entirely underwater in the bathtub?

. . . can you puncture an inflated balloon with a pin, without have it break into pieces?

. . . can you blow up a balloon inside a bottle?

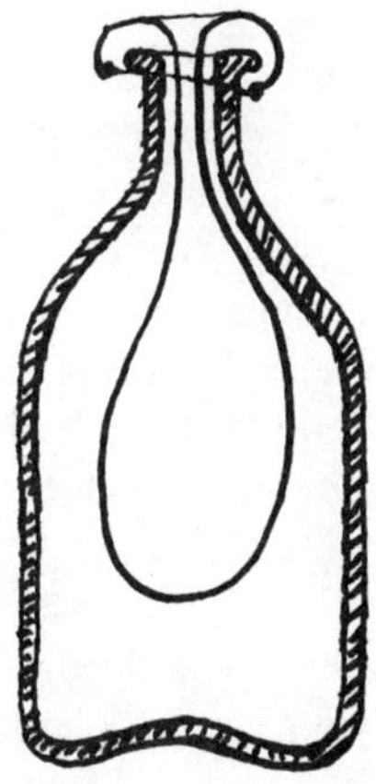

. . . can you blow up one balloon inside another?

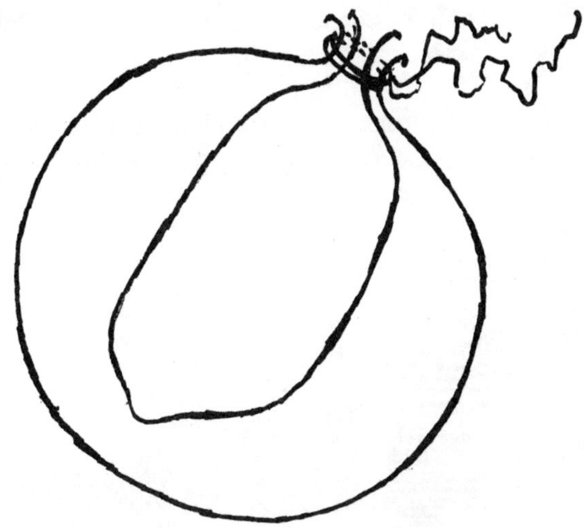

Experiments with balloons

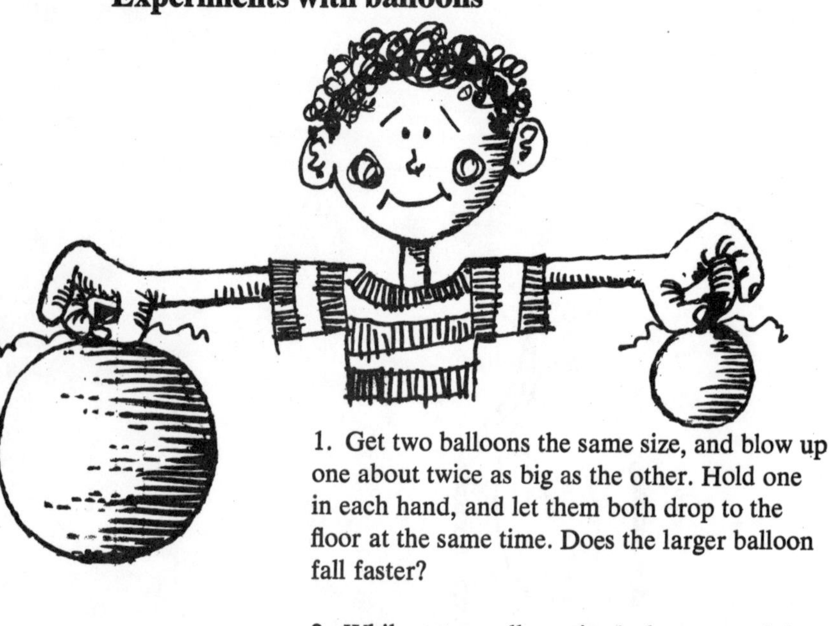

1. Get two balloons the same size, and blow up one about twice as big as the other. Hold one in each hand, and let them both drop to the floor at the same time. Does the larger balloon fall faster?

2. While not usually noticed, there are miniature winds inside your house. These can be detected by dropping balloons and noticing how they fall. Some places where currents might be found are in doorways, near windows and radiators, in front of a fire in the fireplace, and outside the refrigerator when the door is opened.

3. Tie a balloon to a piece of string and hold it against a stream of water from the faucet. What happens?

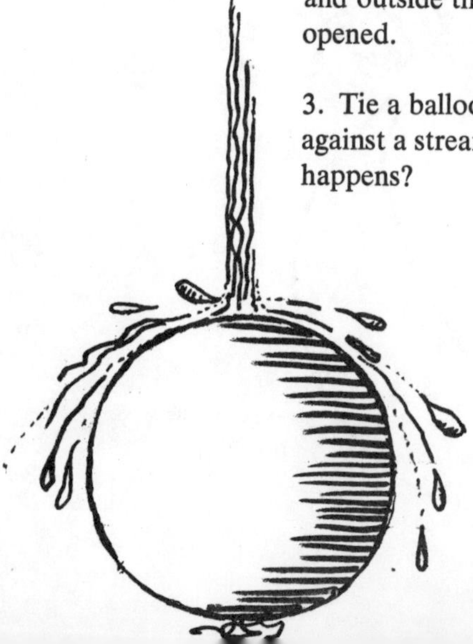

4. You can charge a balloon with static electricity on a cold day by rubbing it on your shirt or a rug. If the balloon has a good charge it will stick to the ceiling. Will the balloon stay on the ceiling for a whole week? Charge two balloons on strings and hold them together. What happens? Hold a charged balloon close to a fine stream of water from a faucet. Does the water stream become bent?

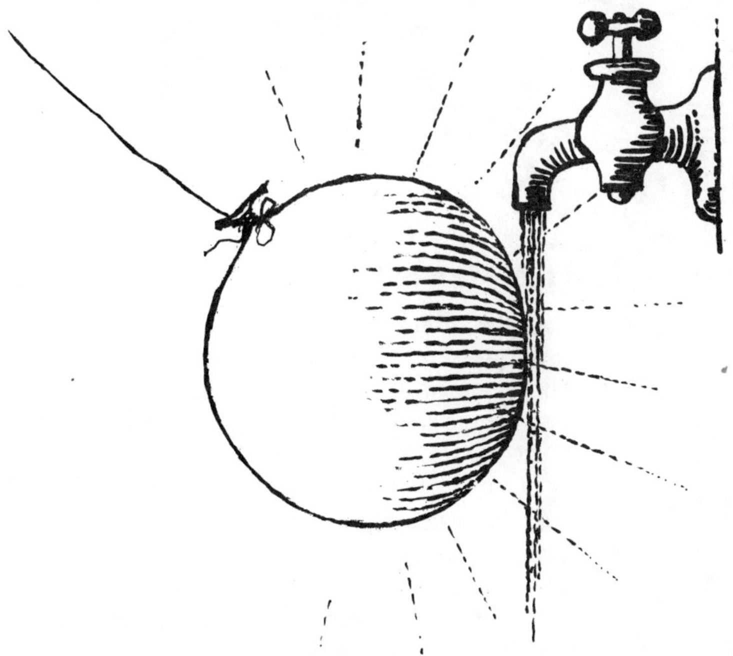

Do all balloons leak?

A balloon full of air very slowly collapses and becomes smaller. Hang a balloon in your room and measure its diameter each day. How quickly does the balloon lose air?
How could you find a way to keep a blown-up balloon from gradually shrinking? Suppose you put several balloons inside of one another? Will a balloon tied under water keep its air? Will a coating of grease help?

Water balloon squirter

Make a pinhole in a large balloon, and place the mouth of the balloon over the bathtub faucet. Turn on the water slowly while supporting the balloon when it fills with water. As the balloon becomes larger, what happens to the stream of water that squirts out of the pinhole?

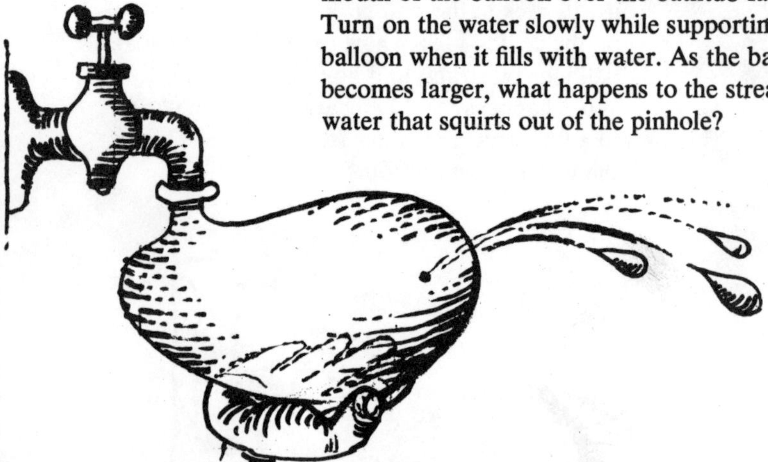

How much air is there in a bike tire?

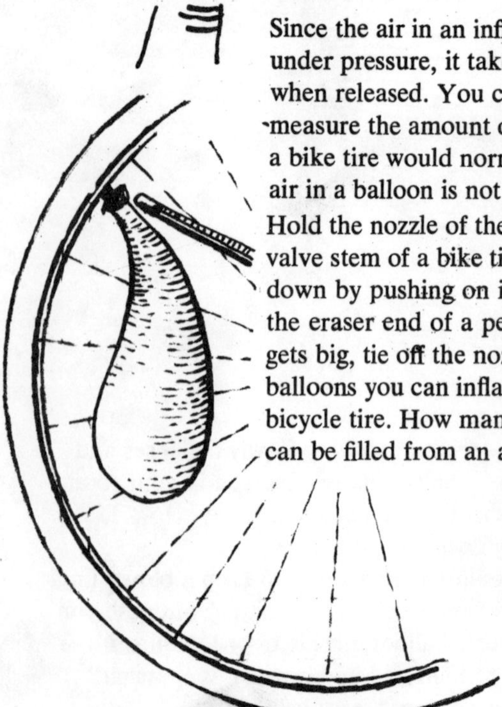

Since the air in an inflated tire is squeezed under pressure, it takes up a lot more space when released. You can use a balloon to measure the amount of space that the air in a bike tire would normally take up, since air in a balloon is not under much pressure. Hold the nozzle of the balloon tightly over the valve stem of a bike tire. Press the valve pin down by pushing on it through the balloon with the eraser end of a pencil. When the balloon gets big, tie off the nozzle. See how many balloons you can inflate with the air from a bicycle tire. How many balloons do you think can be filled from an automobile tire?

Make a little air car

You have probably heard of air-cushioned floating vehicles. You can easily make a frictionless puck with a balloon, a spool, and a disc of thin Masonite. The drawing shows how to put together a simple puck.

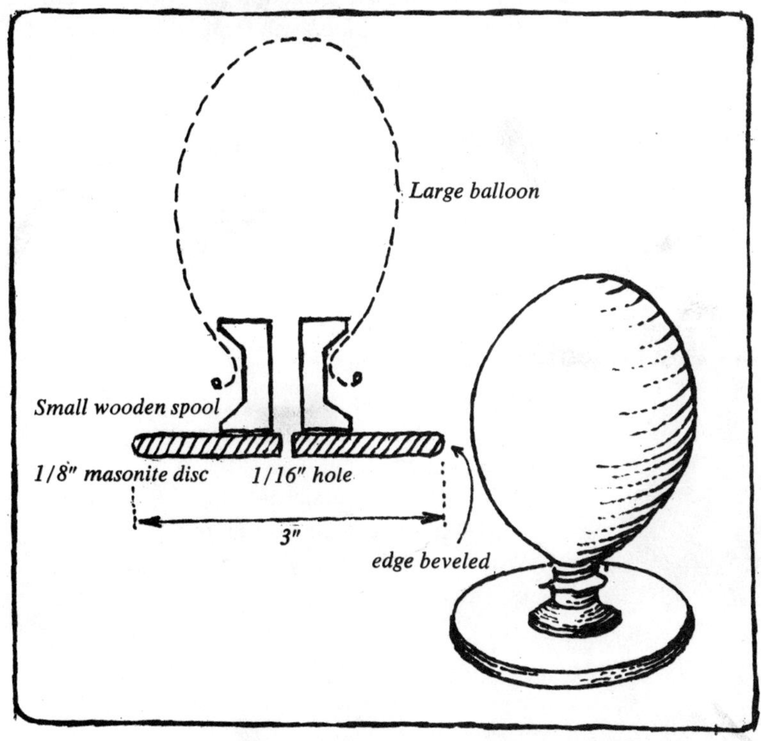

Blow up the balloon through the hole in the bottom of the puck, and cover the hole with your finger to keep the air inside. Place the puck on a smooth table and give it a slight push. It should continue floating just above the table top until the balloon runs out of air. How can you use the puck to see whether tables and floors are level? What happens to the speed of a puck as it slides down an incline? What happens when one puck collides with another one?

For science experts only

. . . A balloon always bursts when pricked by a pin. Why doesn't the air just leak out of the balloon slowly through the pinhole?

. . . If you have a balloon filled with helium in a car, the balloon will float *backward* when the brakes are put on. Can you explain why the balloon does this, while everything else in the car goes forward when the car suddenly stops?

. . . A balloon filled with helium was floating on a string outdoors. Then it started to rain, and the balloon fell to the ground. Why?

Take a balloon in swimming

Will it hold you up?

Can you push the balloon completely underwater?

Will the balloon jump out of the water when you let it go near the bottom of the pool?

What happens when you break the balloon underwater?

5 can you do it?

Straws

Hold two straws in your mouth, but put only one of them into a glass of water. Can you drink any water?

Hold fifteen straws in your mouth and put them into a glass of water. Can you get a drink? Can you drink through a straw that has a pinhole in the middle?

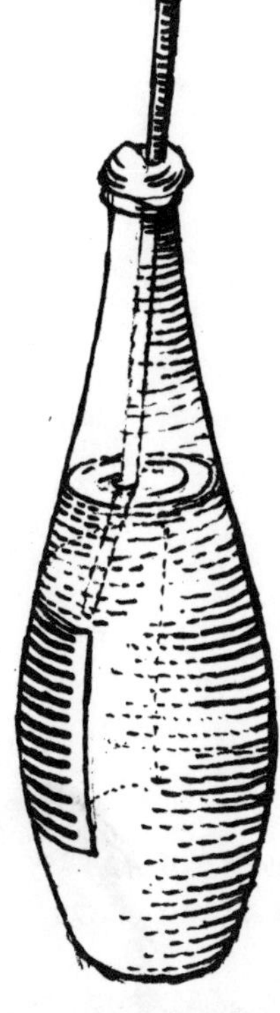

Fill a soda bottle with water and put a straw into it. Then take some clay and pack it into the bottle opening around the straw. Now can you drink any water through the straw?

Can you make a hunk of modeling clay float?

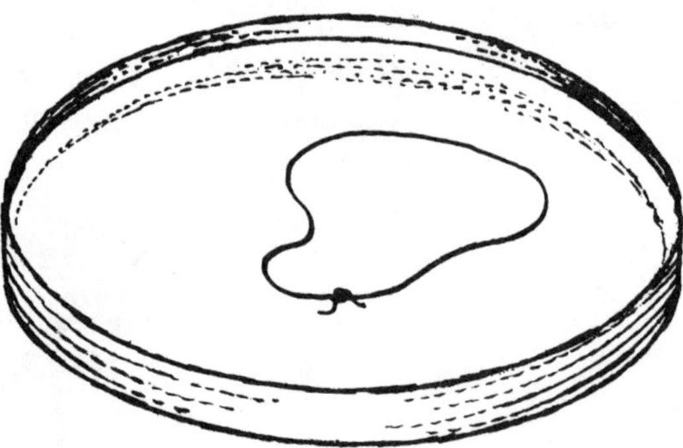

Tie a short piece of thread to make a loop, and float it in water. What can you do to make the loop into a perfect circle without even touching it?

Can you fold a piece of paper in half nine times? Try very thin paper or an extra large sheet.

Can you throw a ball and make it come right back to you without allowing it to hit anything?

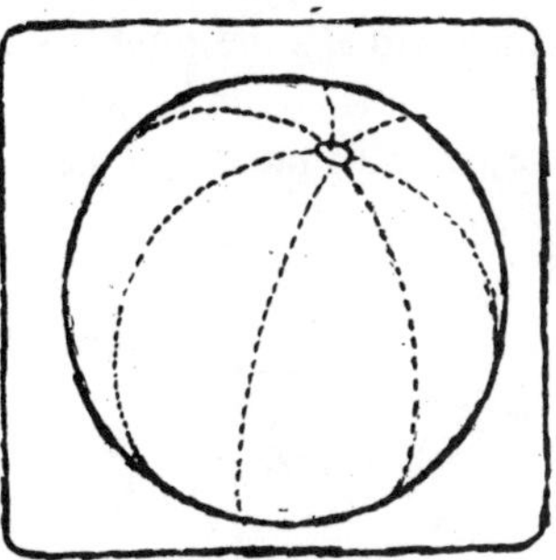

Can you drop a coin onto a flat surface so it stays on its edge for a few seconds?

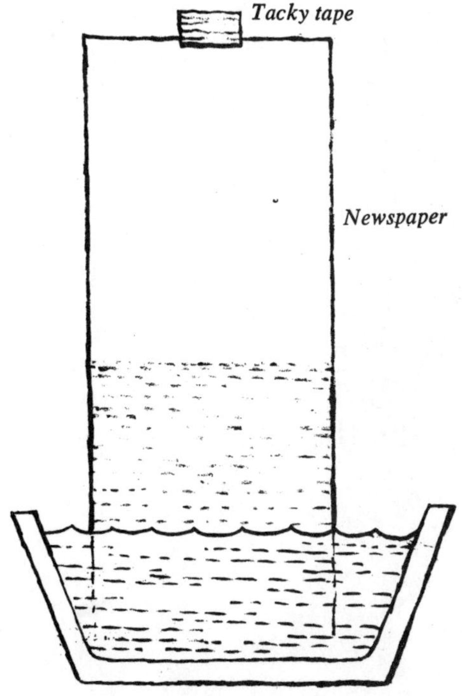

Can you make water climb up a strip of newspaper more than four inches above the water?

36

Mirrors

Can you print your name so that its reflection in a mirror reads the right way?
Look at a friend in a mirror. Can you ever see your friend's face when he cannot see yours?

Can you use two mirrors to make ten reflections of your eye? Try it with a hand mirror and the bathroom mirror.

6 freezing and melting ice

How did the icicle get to the middle of the wire?

What caused frost to form in this curved pattern on the car's windshield?

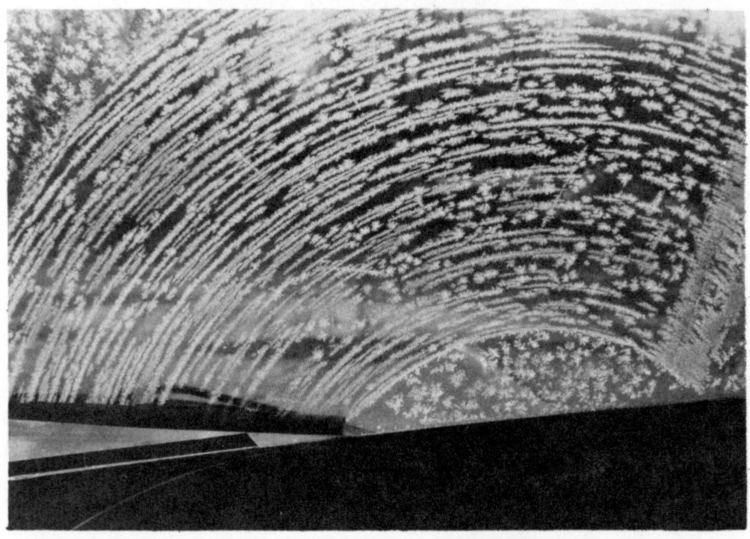

Freezing experiments

1. Fill jars with water as shown, and put them in a freezer. Which of the jars will be broken when the water freezes?

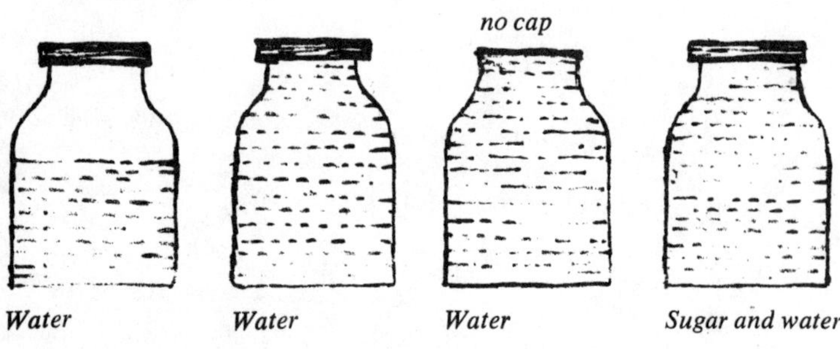

2. What will happen if you try to freeze sea water? The water in the ocean contains about 3 per cent salt. To make a 3 per cent mixture of table salt, dissolve 2 teaspoons of salt in a glass of water. Put the salt water in your freezer overnight. Did it freeze?

3. Try freezing some other liquids such as a dish of milk. Will the milk become solid like ice? What does the milk taste like when it is thawed out?

4. You can make your own popsicles from frozen fruit juices. Fill paper cups with orange juice, apple juice, and grape juice. Put a little stick in each cup before putting them into your freezer. What kind of juice makes the best popsicle?

5. What will happen if a thermometer is frozen in ice? Put a glass of water with a thermometer in it into your freezer. Does the ice get colder than 32° F.?

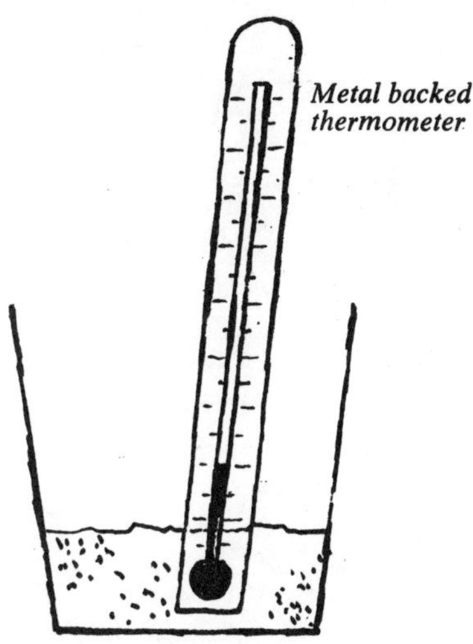

6. How can you make an ice cube of three different colors?

7. Suppose you froze a jar of water that has an ice cube floating in it. Can you still see the ice cube after all the water has turned to ice? Try it.

For freezing experts only

. . . What causes the tops of ice cubes to bulge upward?

. . . Why does a chunk of ice slowly lose weight even when it is kept at a temperature below freezing?

. . . A man in Massachusetts placed a pan of old engine oil behind his garage. A few months later, in December, he looked in the pan and found it filled with ice. Can you explain how this happened?

40
Melting experiments

1. Which cube will melt fastest?

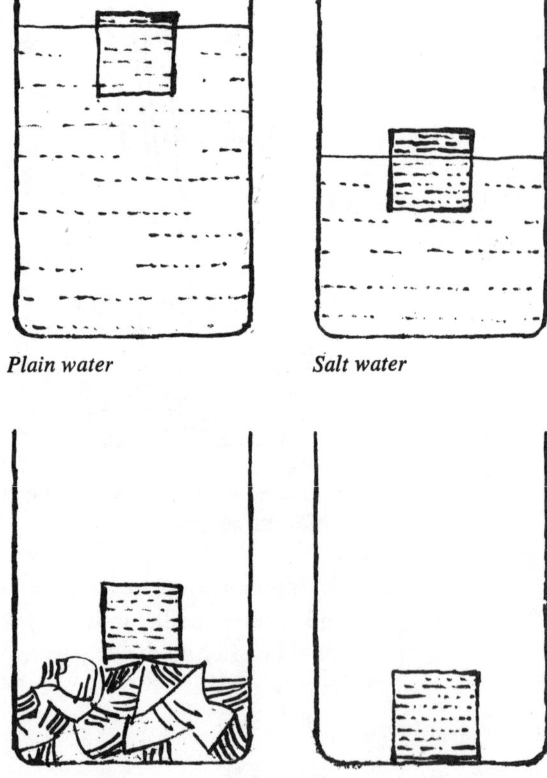

Plain water *Salt water*

Crumpled paper

2. Will an ice cube in an empty glass last overnight in your refrigerator (not your freezer)?

3. Put ice cubes outside on some dirt, on a rock, on the top of a car, and on the street. In what order will the cubes melt? Why don't they all melt at the same speed?

4. If an ice cube is placed in a glass of salad oil or cooking oil, it will sink to the bottom. What will happen as the ice melts? Where will the water go?

5. Put an ice cube into a small strainer and hang it over a pan on the floor. As the ice cube begins to melt, count how many drops of water drip into the pan in a minute. When the ice is almost all melted, will the water be dripping slower, faster, or about the same?

For melting experts only

. . . An ice cube is placed in a cup and balanced with a weight on a balance scale. What will happen to the scale as the ice melts?
. . . Will air from a fan make an ice cube melt faster, slower, or almost the same?
. . . What freezes as it melts?

Explain how this unusual snow-and-soil "mushroom" was formed.

Why has the ice melted near the pilings?

7 water

Some of the plastic globes were filled with water and others have just air. Water was also put into two of the box sections. Which globes and which box sections contain water?

Did you know it is possible to boil water in a paper cup? Try it with a candle and a paper cup of water. Why doesn't the paper burn?

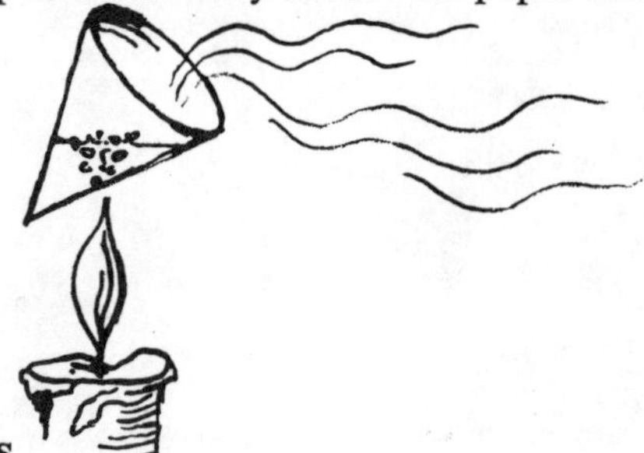

Evaporation races

Dip your hand into water and wet a large circle on the school chalkboard. Draw a line with chalk around the area that is wet. As the water evaporates around the edges, the wet spot will become smaller and smaller. After a minute, draw a second line around the wet spot. Continue doing this each minute until all the water is gone. Why does the wet spot evaporate faster along the top than it does at the bottom? Does the spot change size faster when it is big or small?

Can you find a liquid that will evaporate faster than water? Place a drop of different liquids on a piece of wax paper or aluminum foil. Try such things as vinegar, alcohol, milk, cough syrup, tomato soup, and orange juice. Look at the drops every hour to see which ones have dried up.

For science experts only

. . . How can you keep a drop of water from evaporating?
. . . Will fresh water evaporate faster than salt water?
. . . What causes the dirty spots that are left when water drops evaporate from clean glass?

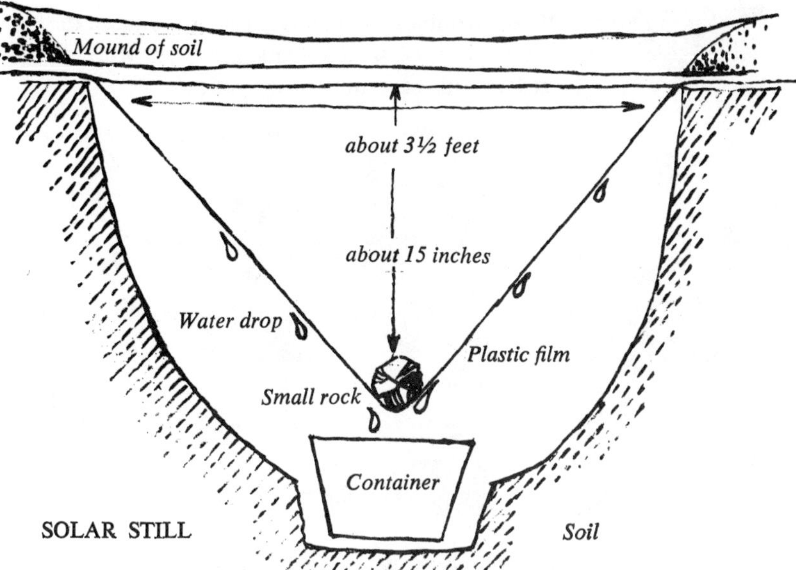

Here is how to make a simple *still* that uses the sun's heat to collect drinking water in dry areas. You must dig a pit about four feet wide and three feet deep. Clear plastic is stretched over the hole, and a small rock placed in the center to form a cone over the container on the bottom. Heat from the sun evaporates water in the soil. The moisture then condenses on the underside of the plastic, and slowly drips into the pan.

Water has condensed on the inside of the watch crystal. Can you explain why the moisture took this pattern?

Water from a faucet runs through the piece of screen, but the screen floats. How can you explain this seeming contradiction?

The photo shows how a cube-shaped wooden block floats in water. The long block leaning against the bowl was made by gluing two cubes together. In what position would the long block float?

Can you do it?

Can you float a needle in a glass of soapy water?

Can you dissolve a drop of oil in a glass of water?

The jar in the mystery photo contains oil, a melting ice cube, and drops of water from the ice. Why does the ice float in the oil if the water sinks to the bottom?

Floating water on water

Make some colored water by mixing a little food coloring into a glass of hot water. Then get another glass half full of cold water. Using a medicine dropper or straw, slowly put the colored hot water on the surface of the cold water. Does some of the hot water float on top or does it become mixed up in the cold water? Continue to add hot water carefully until it is about an inch deep. Can you see a layer of colored water on top? What happens as the hot water cools off?

Now try to put cold water on top of hot water. Add colored cold water to a glass of clear hot water. What happens this time? Can you see any little currents?

What will happen if?

Suppose nail holes were punched into the cans of soda at the places marked by arrows. Out of which holes will soda flow?

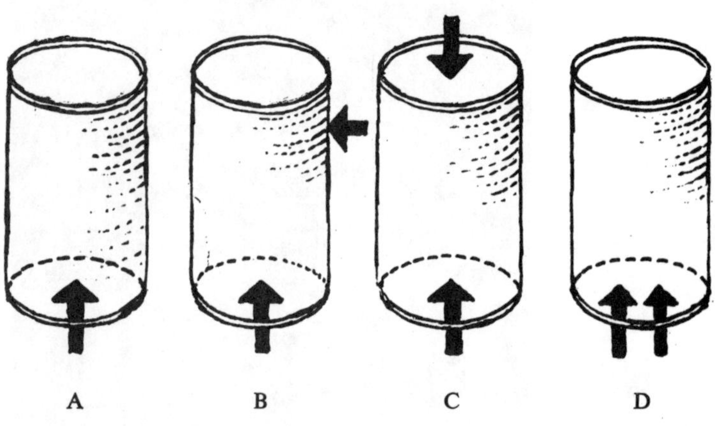

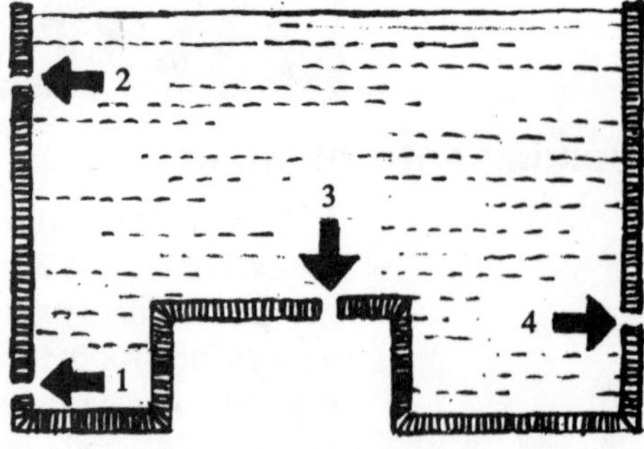

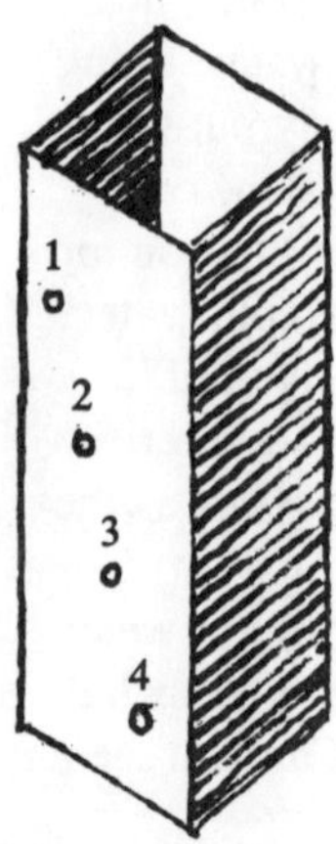

The odd-shaped can has four holes marked by arrows. From which hole would water squirt the fastest?

Punch holes in a milk carton at the four places shown. Place the carton on the ground and fill it with water. From which hole will water squirt the fartherest?

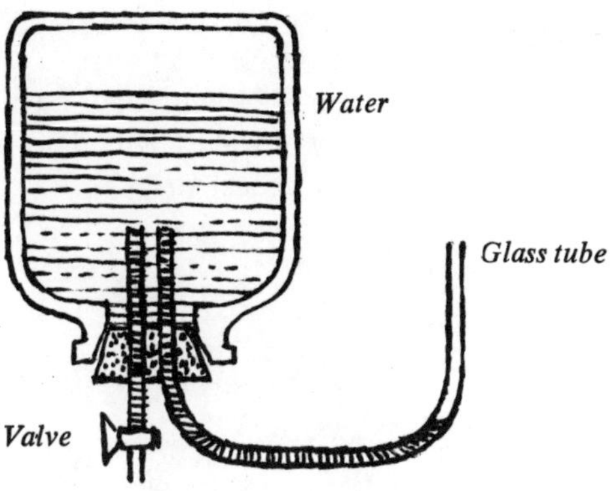

What would happen if the valves were opened?

Where will the water be when the siphons stop?

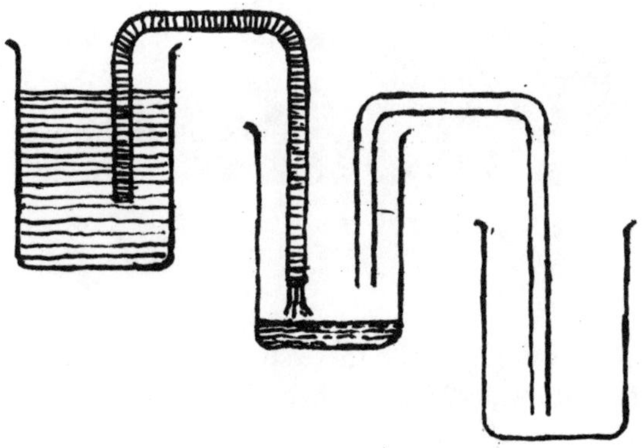

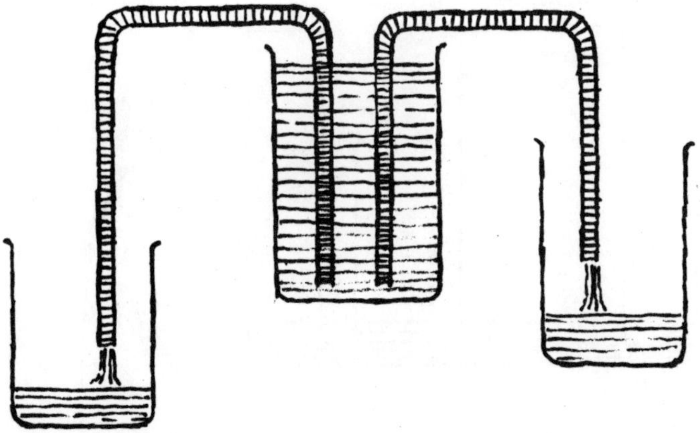

50

Climbing water

Strips of blotter paper have been dipped into a tray of water. Why does the water rise highest in the widest strips?

What will happen to these strips of paper when put into water? Guess, then try it.

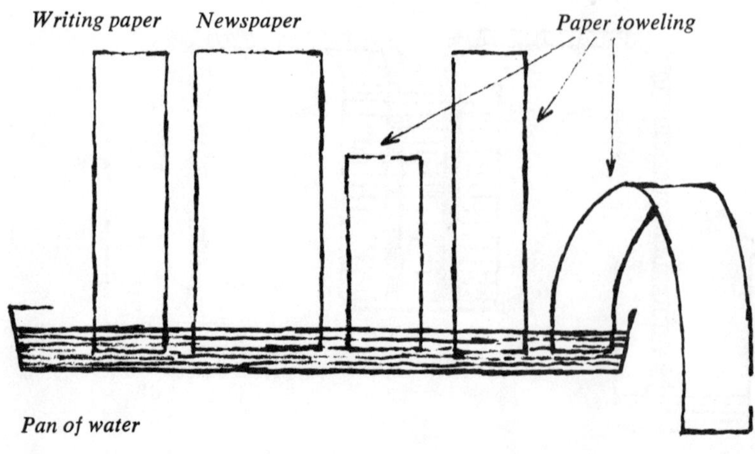

Cooling water

What temperature would result when the water was mixed together?

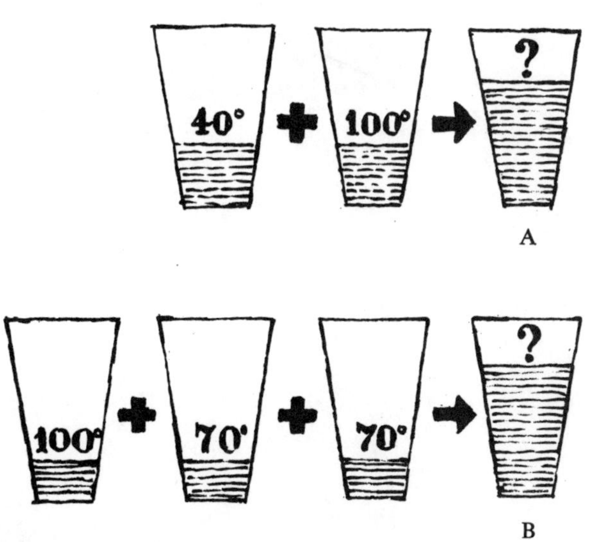

These glass containers each contain a cup of hot water. Which one will cool off fastest?

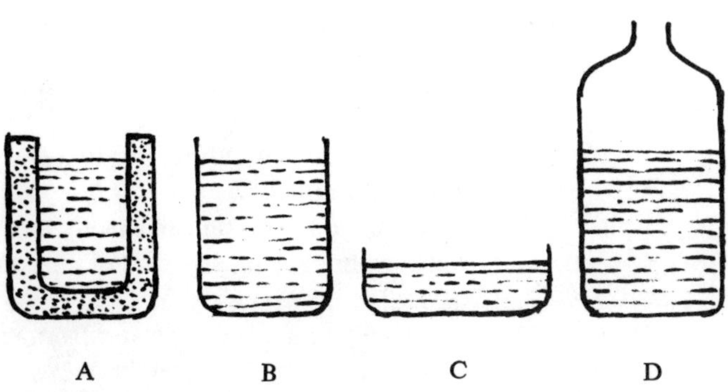

The photograph shows a burning candle floating in a glass of water. A pin has been pushed into the bottom of the candle to make it float straight. Why does the flame seem to be detached from the rest of the candle?

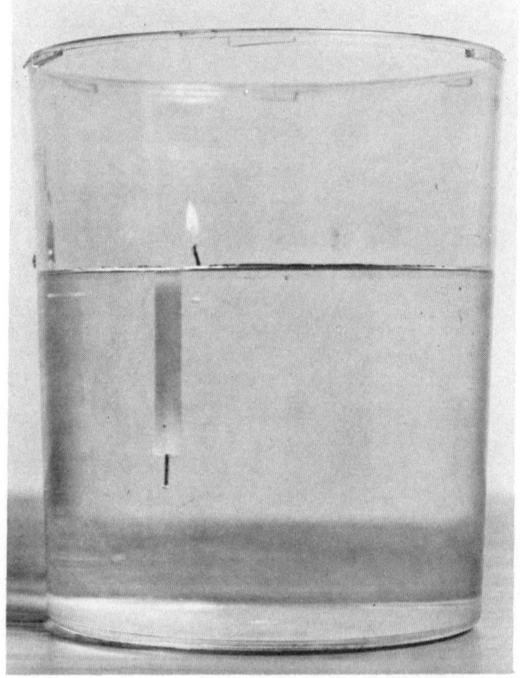

Can you do it?

. . . Can you fill a glass with air while it is held underwater?

. . . Can you add more water to a glass that is already brimful?

. . . Can you get a tin can exactly half full of water without using any kind of measuring device?

. . . Can you make clear water from muddy water without using a filter?

8 fun with shapes

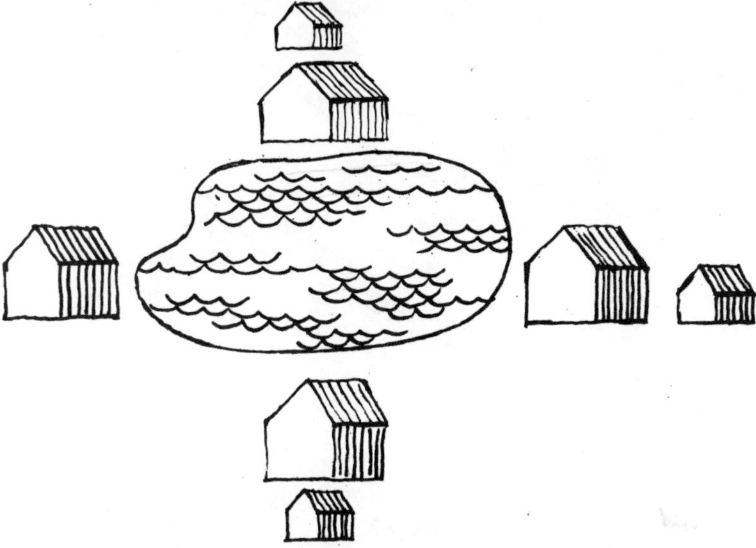

Around the lake are four big houses and four little houses. The people in the little houses want to build a fence to keep the people in the big houses away from the lake. But the people in the little houses want to be able to get to the lake themselves. Draw a line to show how one fence could be built to do this.

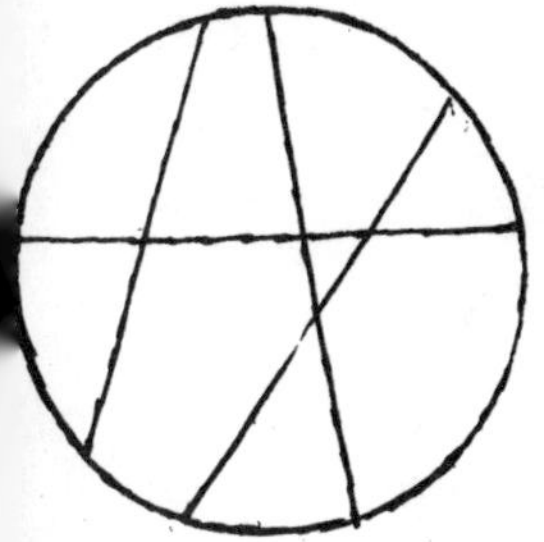

Four lines have been drawn to divide the circle into nine parts. Can you divide a circle into eleven parts with four straight lines? Can you divide a circle into sixteen parts with five lines?

How can you divide a circle into three equal areas using a ruler and a pair of compasses? Can you cut up a cube into three equal pieces without using a ruler to measure? Each piece should be the same shape and have only five faces.

How many surfaces has a piece of paper?

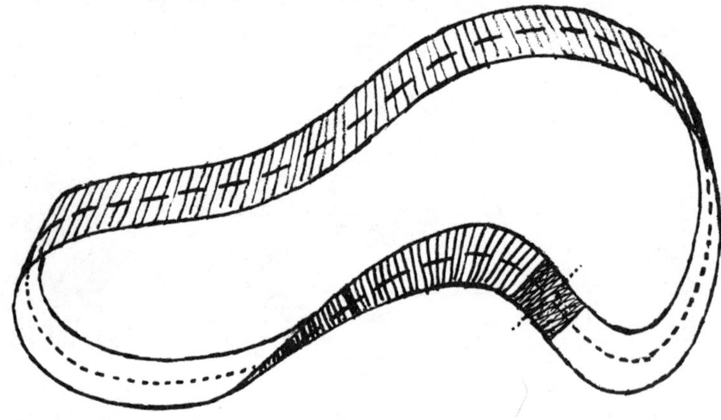

Make a loop of paper with a half twist. Then cut the strip apart along the dashed line. Do you get two loops?

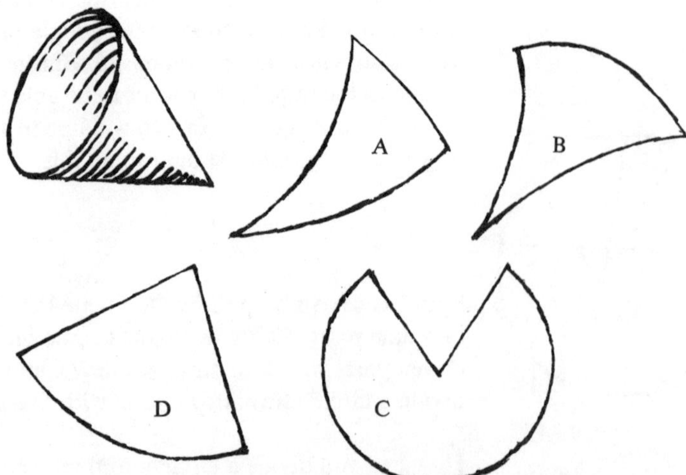

Which piece of paper is the shape used to make a pointed paper cup?

What is the shape of an untwisted cardboard tube from a roll of paper towels?

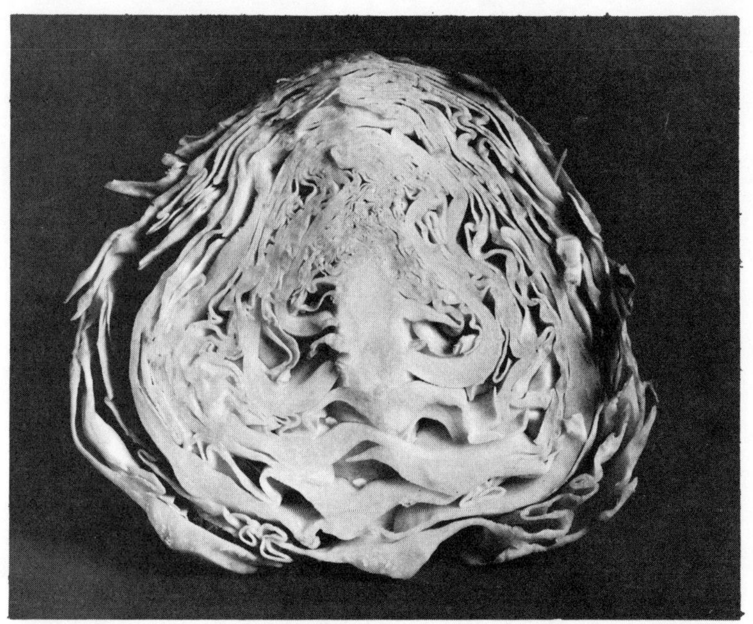

What is it?

If you cut an onion in half one way, it looks like this. What will an onion look like if you cut it in half the other way?

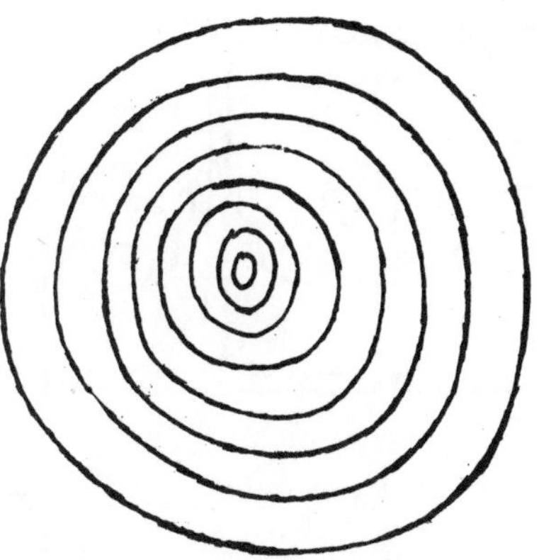

What fruits would look the same regardless of which way you cut them in half?

Trace the design shown without crossing a line or going over the same line twice.

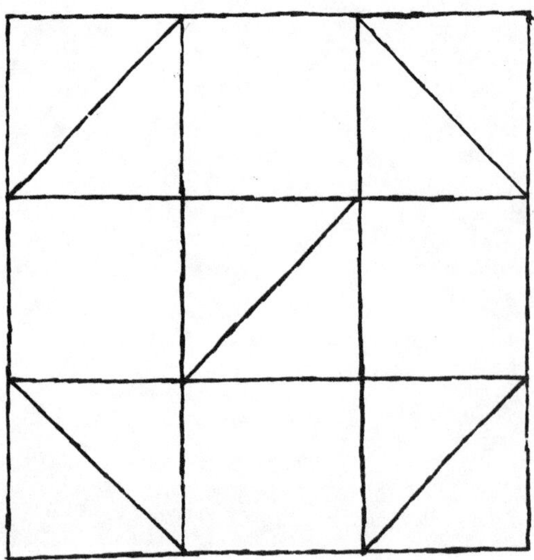

The thirteen sections of fence have been arranged to make separate pens for six pigs. Can you find a way to make six pig pens with only twelve sections of fence?

Arrange eight sugar cubes so that each one is the end of a line of three.

How many different squares are there?

Remove eight toothpicks so that three squares are left.

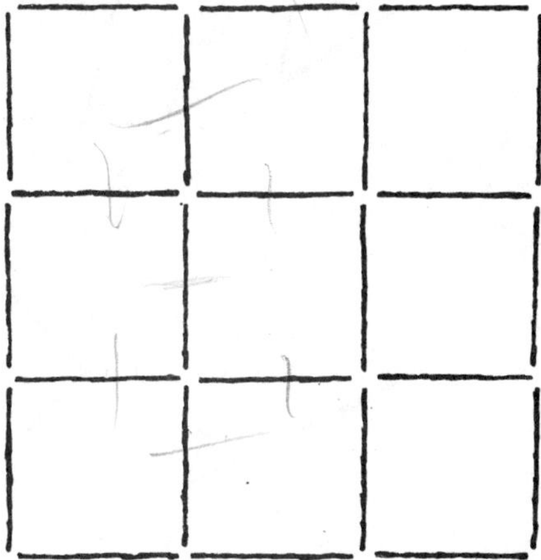

Count the number of lines in the figure shown.

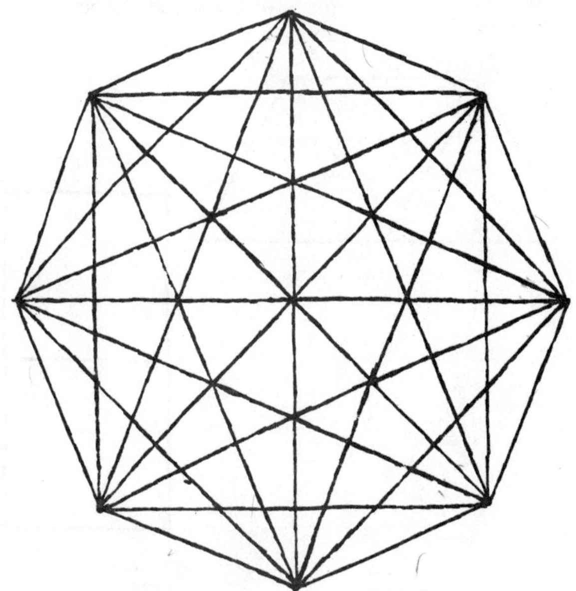

Arrange these four shapes to make a "T."

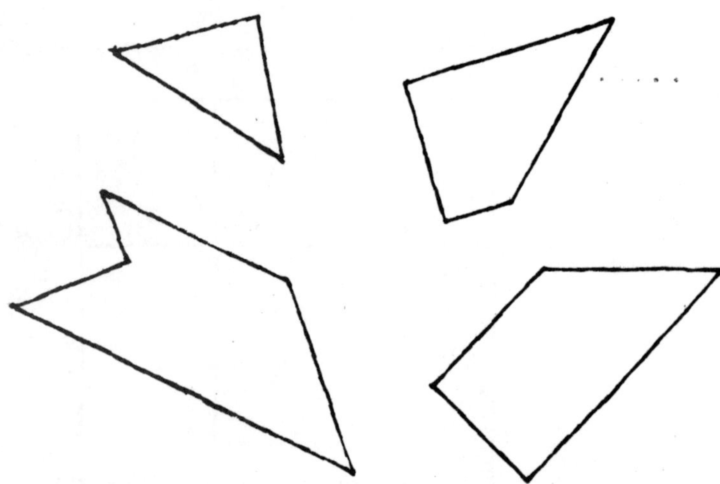

Each of these two designs has been divided into three equal parts of the same shape. Can you divide each of the designs into four equal parts of the same shape?

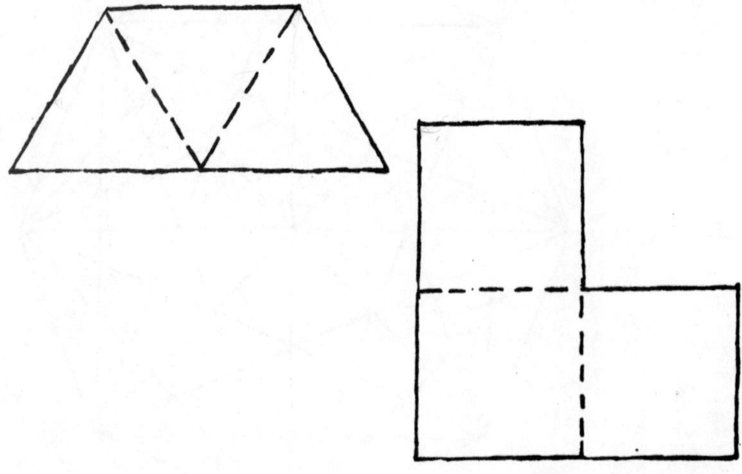

What symbol should be in the empty corner space?

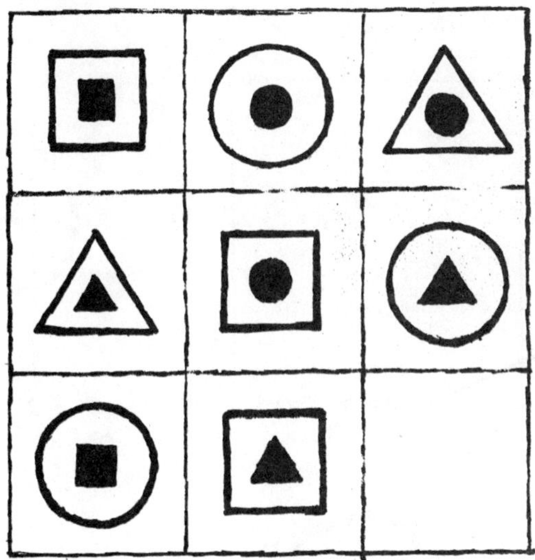

Which of these rings must be cut to make all the rings come apart?

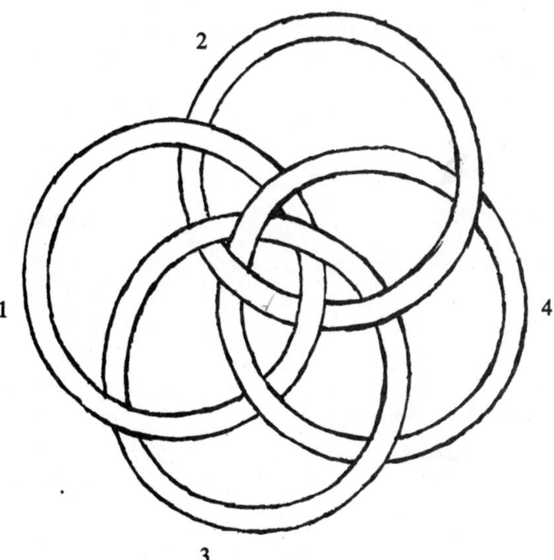

Here is how to cut a six-sided snowflake out of paper.

1. Start with square piece of paper

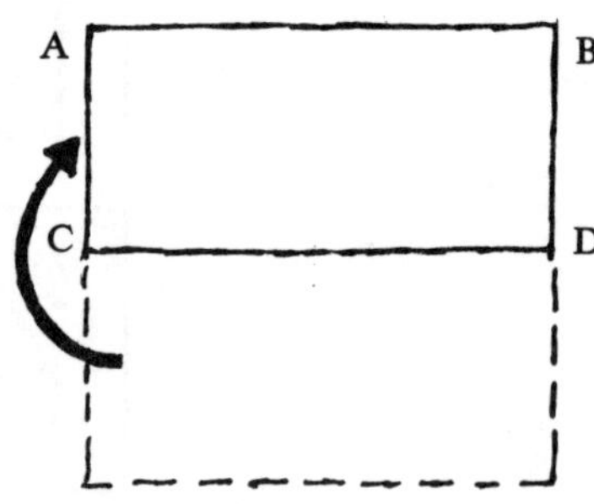

2. Fold it in half

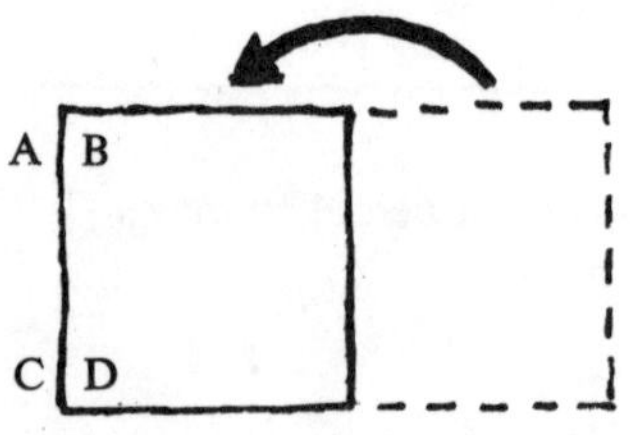

3. Fold it again

4. Fold it again

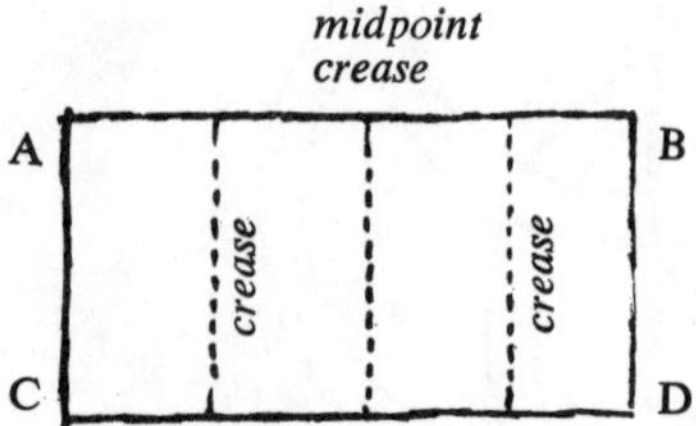

5. Unfold steps 3 and 4

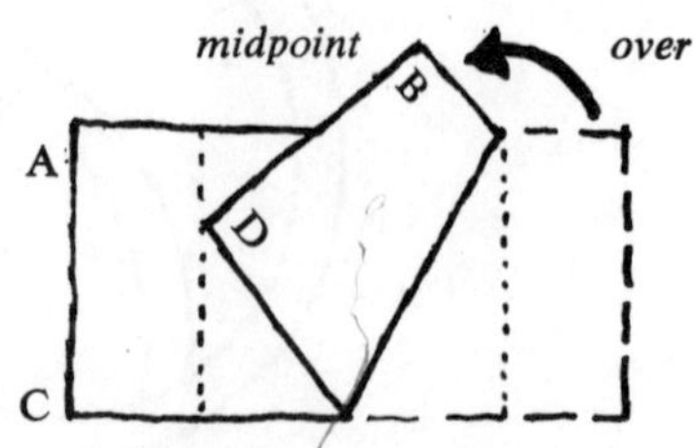

6. Now fold corner D up on top like this

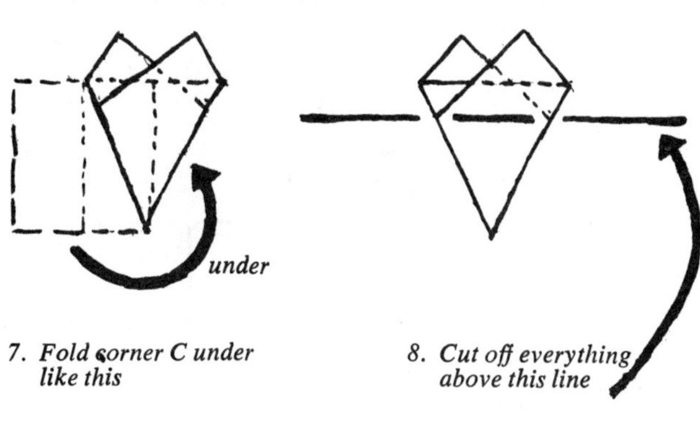

7. Fold corner C under like this

8. Cut off everything above this line

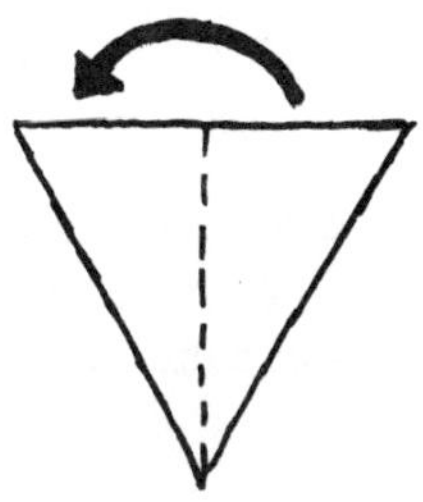

9. Fold in half on dotted line

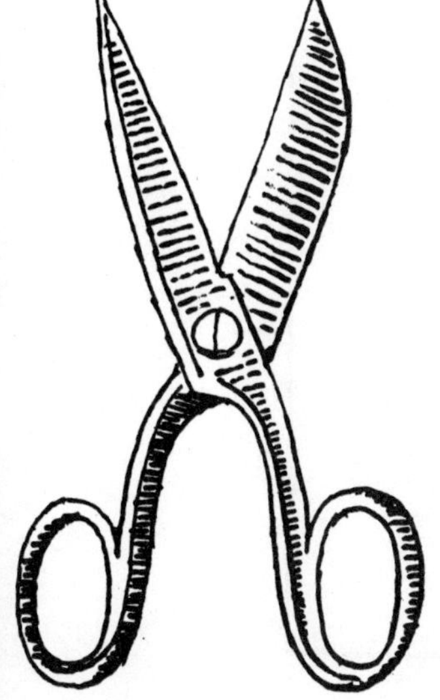

main fold

10. Cut pattern as shown in shaded areas and remove

11. Unfold what is left and see a snow flake

How can you cut the cross into pieces that can be fitted together to make a square? Trace the cross on paper, cut it out, and then cut it up into pieces.

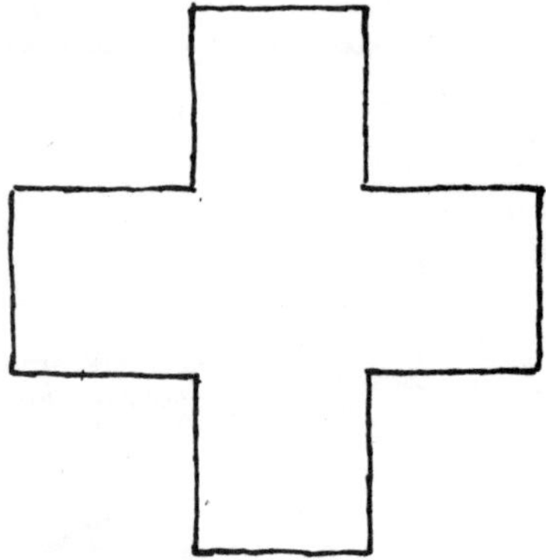

A piece of paper was folded and punched just once with a paper punch. How can you fold and punch a piece of paper so it looks like the drawing when unfolded?

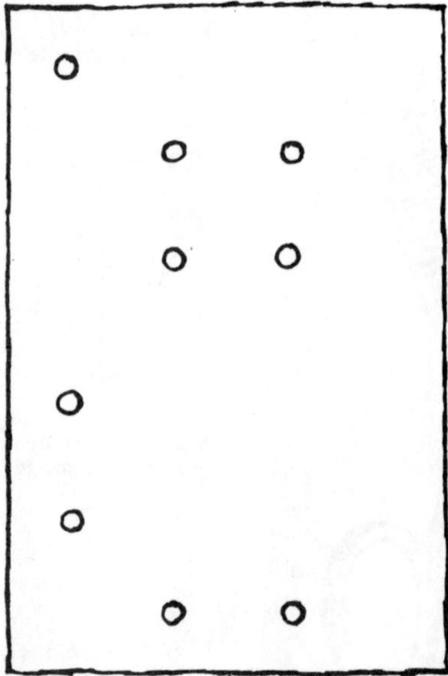

9 why is it made this way?

Many balls have curved lines on them like those on the soccer ball, baseball, and basketball. Do you know why?

Why does a golf ball have dimples?

Why is a paper straw made with a spiral seam instead of a cheaper, straight seam?

Why do most pencils have six flat sides, instead of a cheaper, round shape?

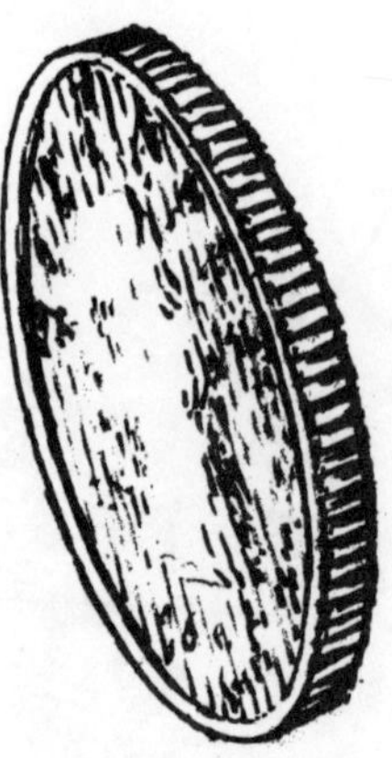

Why do dimes and quarters have knurled edges, instead of a cheaper, smooth edge?

Why are these milk bottles rectangular instead of round like most other glass bottles?

Why does this plastic oil bottle have such an unusual shape?

Why is the roof crooked instead of flat?

Why are the beams sticking out of the wall?

Why were the spaces left in the bridge railing?

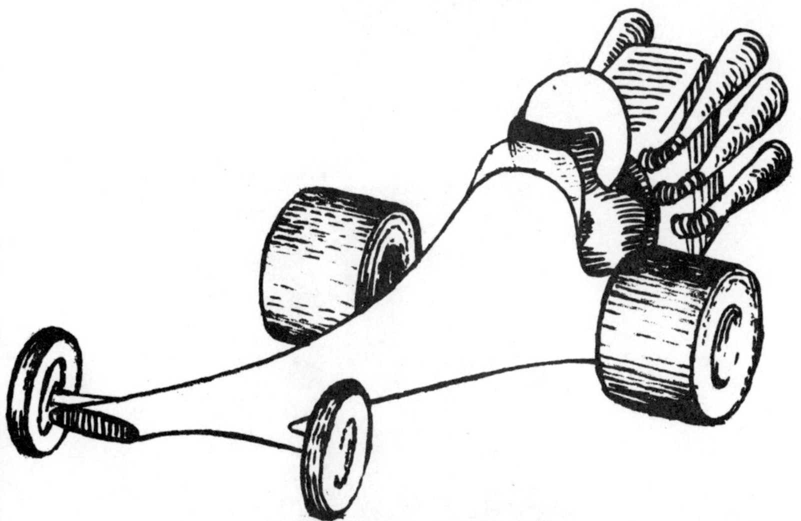

If the tread on a tire helps to increase friction, why are the tires of drag racers usually bald?

Why are the towers on suspension bridges so high? It would be much cheaper if they could be made shorter.

What was the large tank used for?

10 noise

Here is how to make a hose trombone. Put a bend as shown in a garden hose that has some water in it. By lifting the end of the hose up and down, you can make the water level rise and fall. This will change the length of the air column inside the hose. If you blow across the open end of the hose, you will hear a sound that is higher or lower, depending on the length of the air column. How does shortening the air column change the sound?

You can make a little horn with a paper straw. Squeeze together one end and snip off the corners. Put one inch of the cut end into your mouth and blow.
Can you make a noise? What happens to the sound as you cut the straw shorter and shorter?

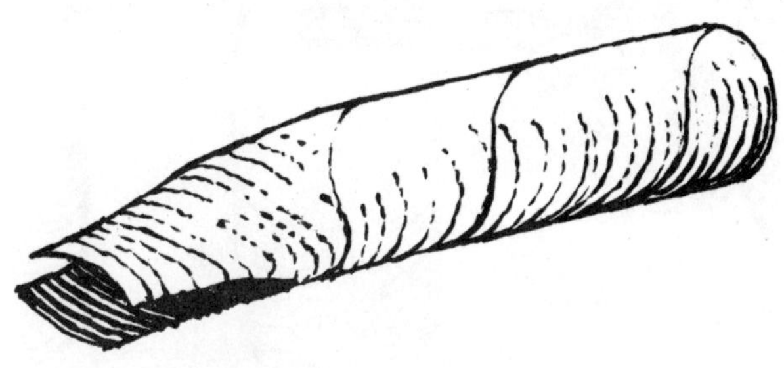

You can make a speaker for a record player from a paper cone and a pin. Put an old record on a moving record player, and hold the pin point in the groove. Can you hear anything? See if you can feel the vibrations by lightly touching the pinhead.

Pour different amounts of water into two bottles of the same size and shape. Then blow across the top of each bottle. Which bottle makes a higher note? Now tap the bottles with a pencil. Does the same bottle give the higher note?

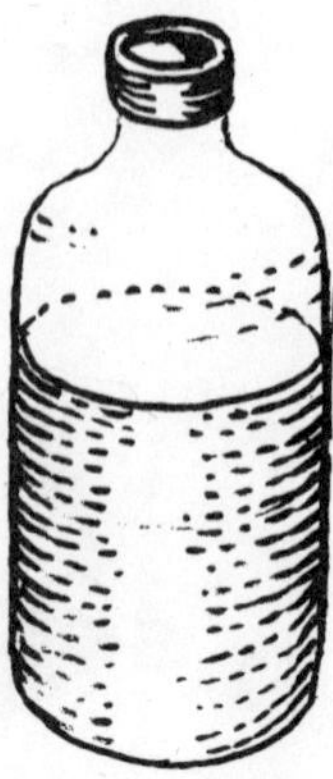

Can you do it?

What can you do to hear a watch tick when it is three feet away from your head?

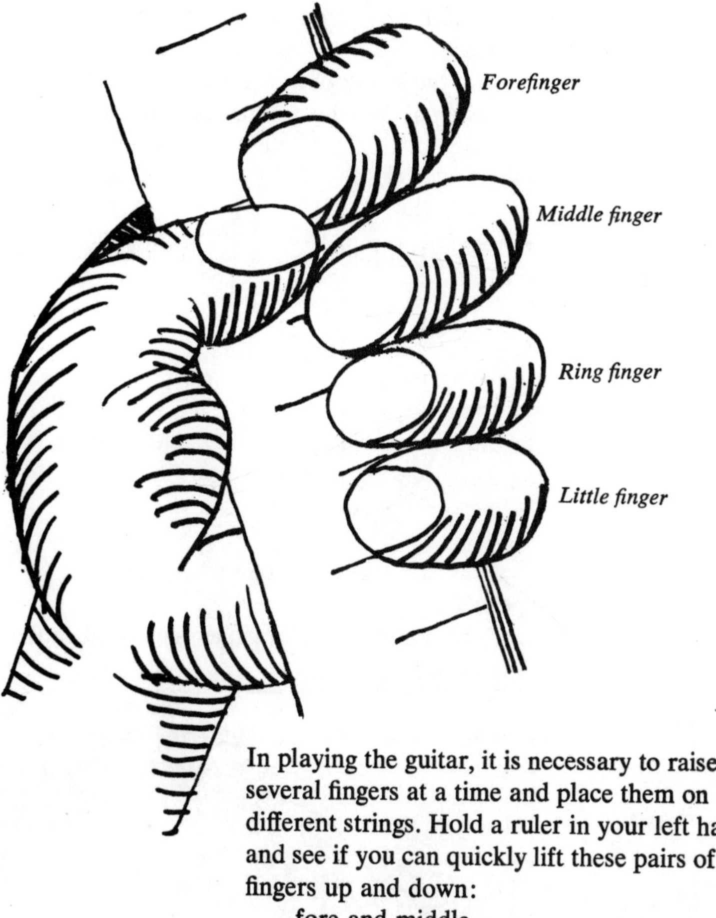

In playing the guitar, it is necessary to raise several fingers at a time and place them on different strings. Hold a ruler in your left hand and see if you can quickly lift these pairs of fingers up and down:

fore and middle
middle and ring
ring and little
fore and little
fore and ring
middle and little

Were you able to do all of them? Which pair was the hardest? Try it with your right hand, too.

For science experts only

. . . How do astronauts on the moon talk to one another? There is no air to carry sound waves.

. . . If the length of a piano string determines the pitch of the sound it makes, how can pianos of different sizes have the same notes?

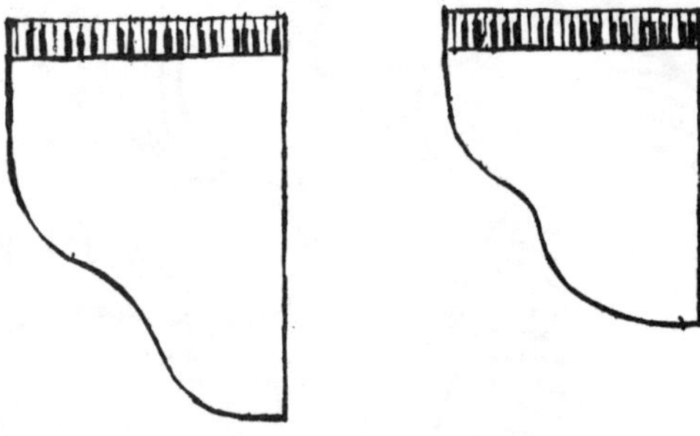

. . . What makes the noise when a balloon pops?

. . . Listen to a glass of ginger ale. What causes the noise?

. . . What makes the sound when you hold an empty glass to your ear?

11 for science experts only

What mammal has the longest life span?
What fruit has its seeds on the outside?
If goldfish have gills to get oxygen from the water, why do they die when they are out of water in the air?

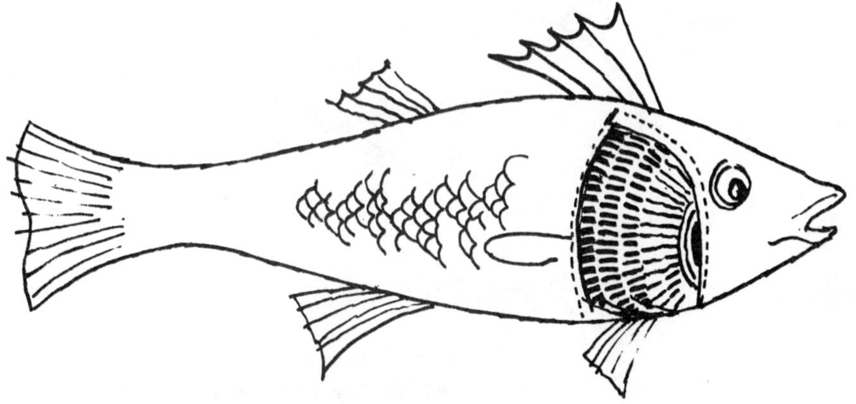

If soil comes from rocks, why is there so little soil on the tops of high mountains?
Suppose you dug a hole straight down into the earth under your house. Where would you come out? Would you be in China, in Australia, or in the Pacific Ocean?

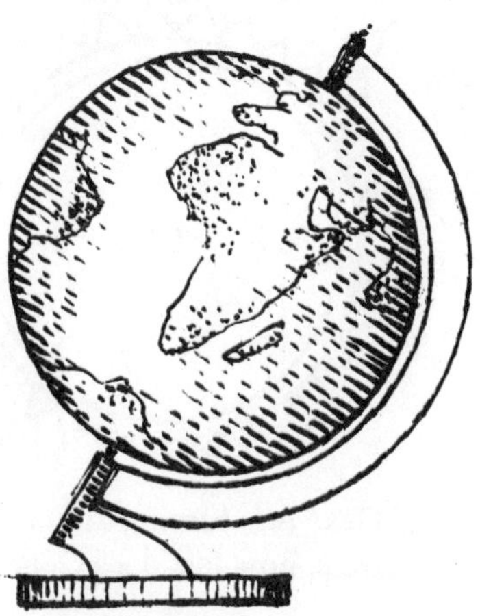

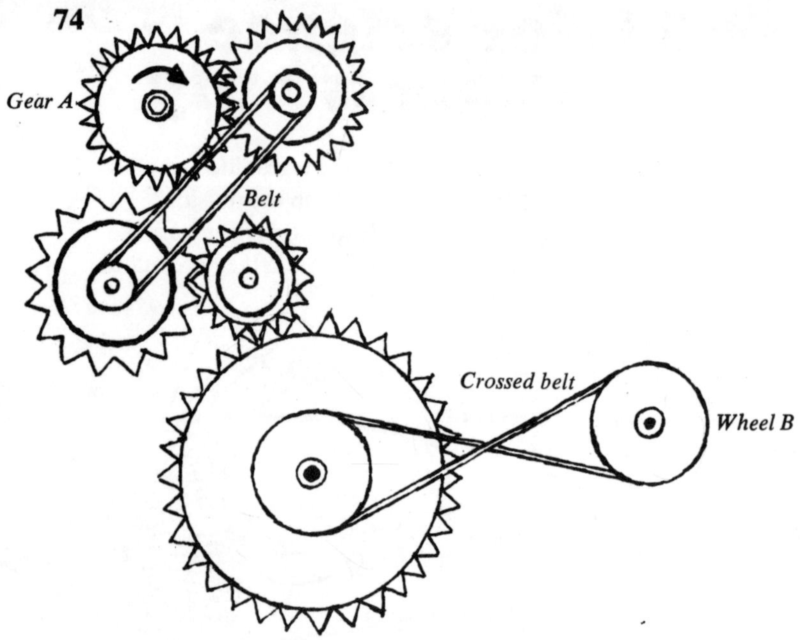

When Gear A is moved in the direction of the arrow, which way does Wheel B move?

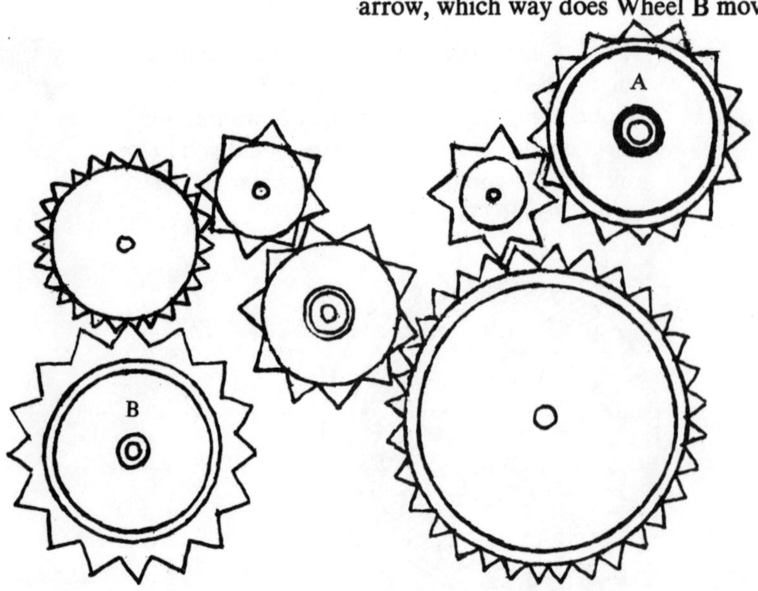

If Gear A is turning around three times per minute, how fast does Gear B turn?

Why does soda shoot out if you shake the can before opening it?

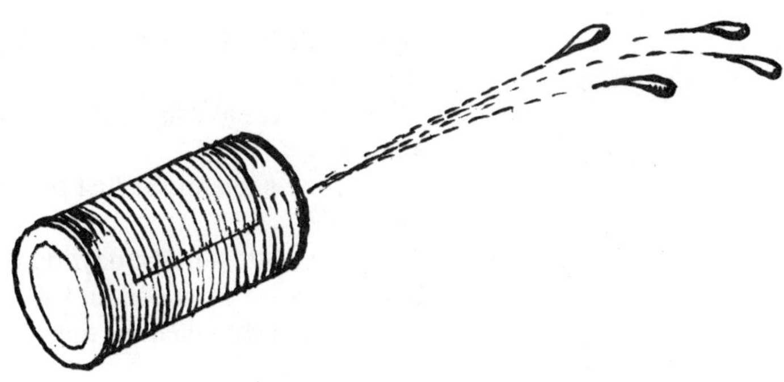

If tin does not rust, why do tin cans rust?
What happens to the weight of a metal tank as helium gas is pumped in? Does the tank's weight increase, decrease, or stay the same?
How small can a mirror be in which you can see yourself from head to toe?

For astronomy experts only

When seen from the earth, which planet looks the biggest?
Which planet has canals, icecaps, and an atmosphere?
What is the name of the first satellite to circle the earth?
Can you see stars in the daytime?
If you were on the moon, in what phase would the earth appear when the moon is full?

Why does the sun appear to be almost round at sunrise, but often seem egg-shaped at sunset?

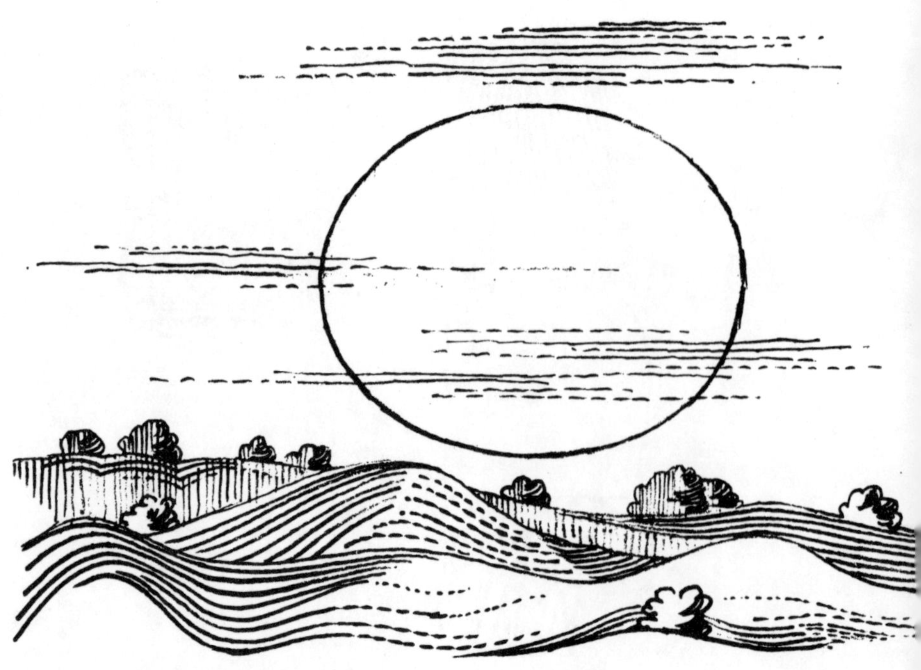

Fire cannot burn without oxygen, and there is no oxygen in space. How, then, can the sun be so hot?

Here are three reasons why many early scientists believed that the earth was not rotating:

1. If the earth were spinning, there would be a continual wind blowing from the direction toward which the earth turned.
2. If the earth were spinning, everything would be thrown off into space because of centrifugal force.
3. If the earth were spinning, a stone thrown straight up into the air would land at a different spot from where it was thrown.

Since the earth really is spinning, can you explain why these things do not occur?

Which way must this propeller spin in order to make the airplane go forward?

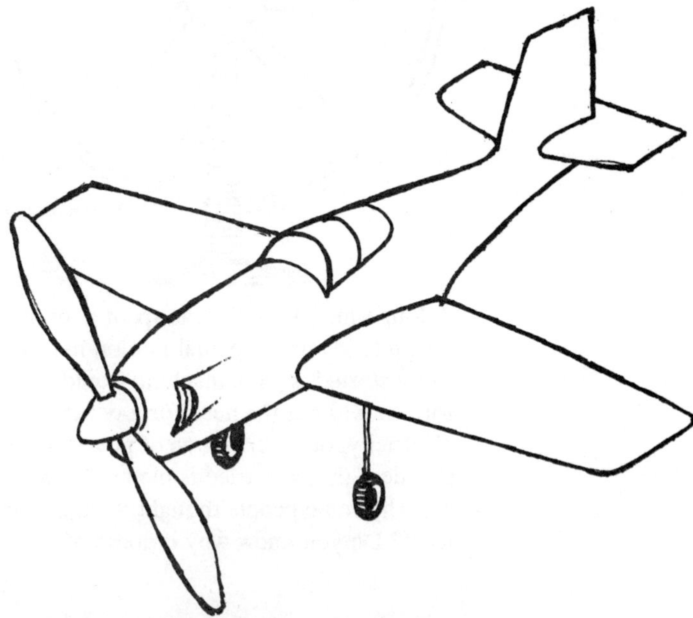

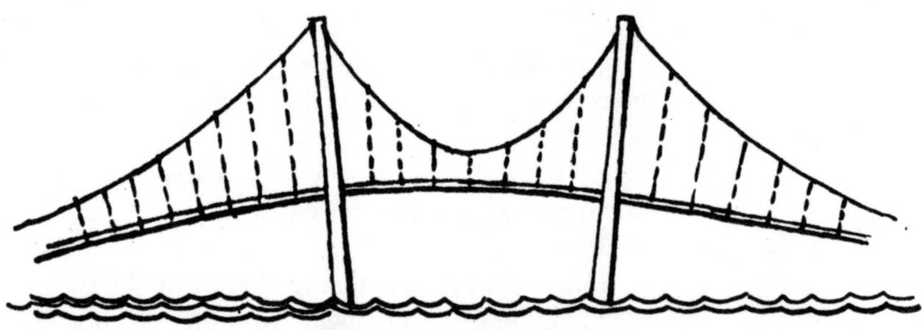

The main span of the Verrazano Bridge connecting Brooklyn and Stäten Island, New York, is about 4/5 of a mile long. Why are the two 800-foot-tall towers that support the span 1 5/8 inches farther apart at the top than at the bottom?

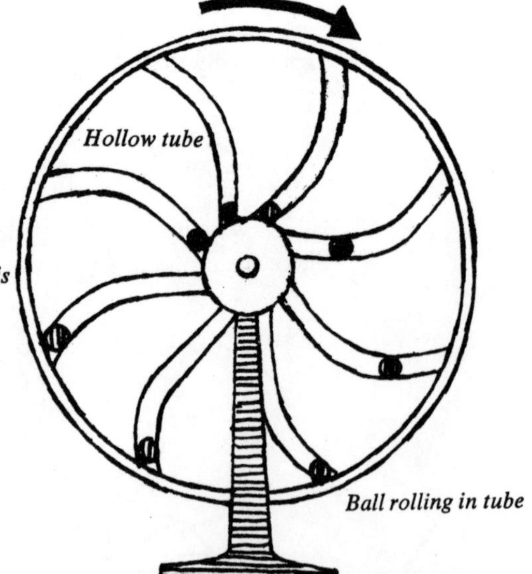

A long time ago, scientists spent a lot of time trying to invent perpetual motion machines. Once started, such a machine would run forever without the need for any fuel, electricity, or other source of power. One of the ideas that was tried is pictured. Can you see why some people thought it would turn by itself? Do you know why it does not?

A man was sentenced to die; but was allowed to decide if he would be hanged or shot. He had to make a statement, and if what he said were true, he would be shot. If he said something that was false, however, he would be hanged. After thinking a moment, the man made a statement that made it impossible for him to be shot or hanged? What did he say?

What we caught we threw away; what we could not catch we kept. What is it?

A king wanted to choose which of two princes could marry his daughter. He decided that there should be a horse race, and told the princes that the one whose horse ran *slower* would be the winner. Neither prince could understand how such a race would be possible. Finally one prince had an idea of how the race could be run. He told the king his plan, and the king then let him marry his daughter. How did the smart prince suggest that the horse race be run?

Can you explain these science contradictions?

The sun is closest to the earth in June, but the warmest days are in July and August.

If heat rises, why is the air in Death Valley (the lowest spot on the North American Continent) so hot in the daytime?

Campers sometimes keep their food cold by putting it in a hole in the ground; yet the temperature in a deep gold mine in South Africa is more than 120° F.

If you left the refrigerator door open, your kitchen would not be cooled off at all.

The lens of a camera makes an image on the film that is upside down. Why is it, then, that photographs are not always upside down?

Pointed nails will split a board more often than blunt nails.

12 kitchen chemistry

Starch

You can use cornstarch to write secret messages. Stir a teaspoon of cornstarch into a glass half full of water. Dip a matchstick into the mixture and use it to print some words on a piece of paper. You must dip the match into the starch mixture after each letter. Allow the letters to dry for about twenty minutes. While you are waiting, add five drops of tincture of iodine to a small glass of water. To make the writing appear, wet the paper with the iodine solution.

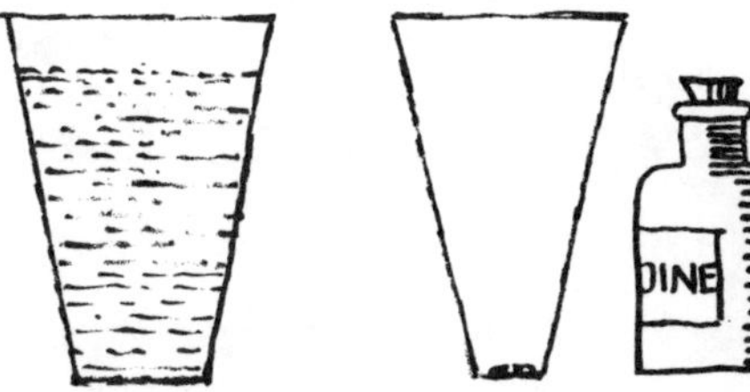

Here is how to perform a trick with starch and tincture of iodine. Place a few drops of iodine in an empty glass. In another glass, mix two tablespoons of cornstarch with water. Show someone the two glasses and say you are going to change milk into ink by pouring it into an empty glass. The "milk," of course, is the white starch mixture, and then the "empty" glass has iodine hidden on the bottom. When the starch water hits the iodine, it darkens and looks like ink.

Put a handful of cornstarch into a dish. Slowly add water, mixing it with the starch until you have a thick paste. The wet starch is a strange substance. It will pour slowly like molasses. And yet if you try to force your thumb into it quickly, the soggy starch seems almost solid.

Vinegar

Vinegar is used to test for limestone. If a piece of limestone is put into vinegar, the vinegar will fizz as hydrogen gas bubbles out. Test rocks, chalk, paper, sea shells, plaster, and other things. How long does the fizzing continue?

Pour a little vinegar into a glass of milk and watch what happens.

Carbon dioxide

Carbon dioxide gas will put out fire. In a large glass make some CO_2 from baking soda and vinegar. Lower a burning match slowly into the invisible gas. What happens to the flame just before it goes out?

A convenient source of carbon dioxide is Alka-Seltzer tablets. Drop one into a glass of water and watch it fizz. How long does it take for the tablet to dissolve completely? What can you do to make a tablet dissolve faster? Break one into small pieces. Drop the pieces into a glass of water at the same time you put a whole tablet into another glass of water. Which tablet disappears first? Will a tablet dissolve faster in a large pan of water? What will happen in warm and hot water? Would a tablet dissolve faster in any other liquids such as salt water, alcohol, or vinegar?

How much CO_2 is produced from one of these tablets? You can measure the volume of gas with a jar of water inverted in a pan of water. Cover a filled jar of water with a stiff piece of paper before turning it upside down in the pan. Slip a tablet under the bottle and watch the CO_2 bubbles. Is there more than a half pint of CO_2 given off?

The oven

Ask your parents if you can try to melt things in the oven. Let it heat up to 500° F. Then put in different substances on a piece of aluminum foil. Try some sugar, soap, salt, wood, metal, paper, solder, and rock. Guess which things will burn and melt, and which will stay the same. Look in the oven after fifteen minutes to see what happened.

Many foods are preserved by drying. You can make dried apples in your oven. Take an apple and remove the skin and core with a sharp paring knife. Then cut up the apple in thin slices. Spread out the slices on aluminum foil in a warm oven. In an hour they should be shriveled but not burned. Taste one, but save the rest to eat in a few months.

How much water is there in lettuce? Get a head of lettuce and weigh it on your bathroom scale. Then spread out the leaves to dry in a warm oven. After several hours, reweigh the leaves when they are completely dry and stiff. About what per cent of the plant is water?

Can you do it?

Can you dissolve more than ten teaspoons of salt in a glass of water?

Mix together a little salt and pepper. Can you now quickly separate the pepper from the salt?

Put five teaspoons of cornstarch into a small cup. Into another small cup put four teaspoons of cornstarch and one teaspoon of baking soda. Now shuffle around the cups so you no longer know which is which. Can you make a test to tell which cup contains the baking soda? You probably won't be able to taste any difference.

How can you make a glass of water that contains exactly one eighth of a drop of milk?

Just for fun

Most people know that pennies can be cleaned with a mixture of salt and vinegar. Catsup can also be used to brighten up pennies. Put some catsup on an old penny and wash it off after a few hours.

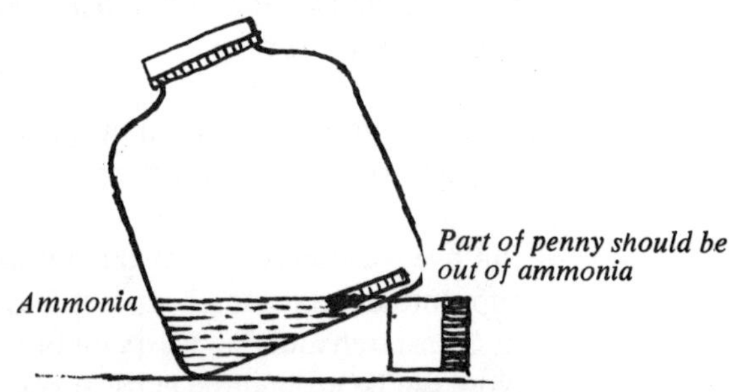

Put a penny into a little household ammonia in a covered jar, as shown. Be careful not to touch or sniff the ammonia. In a short time the ammonia should begin to turn a beautiful shade of blue.

It is easy to burn steel in a candle flame. Get a steel wool pad, pull off a corner, and rinse it in water to wash out the soap. Then, using a pair of tweezers, hold the steel wool in a candle flame. Does the burning steel remind you of a sparkler?

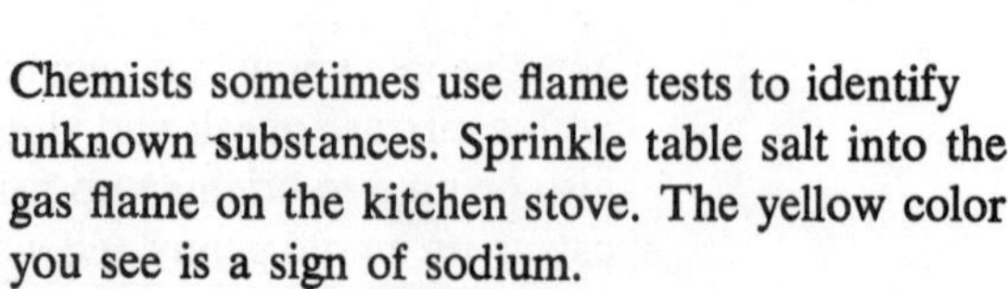

Chemists sometimes use flame tests to identify unknown substances. Sprinkle table salt into the gas flame on the kitchen stove. The yellow color you see is a sign of sodium.

For a colorful mess, put some water, dishwashing liquid, and food coloring into a pan. Then drop in an Alka-Seltzer tablet and watch what happens

13 fun with numbers

Here are the digits from 1 to 9 arranged so they equal 100. Can you find another way to do this?

```
  15
  36
 +47
 ---
  98
 + 2
 ---
 100
```

What rule was followed when these numbers were arranged?

8 5 4 9 1 7 6 3 2 0

What number can be added to 7 or multiplied by 7 to give the same answer?

142857 is an unusual number. Multiply it by each of the numbers from 2 to 7. What do you notice about the answers?
What number is next in each series?

A 1 → 4 → 7 → 10 → ?

B 1 → 2 → 4 → 8 → 16 → ?

C 1 → 3 → 4 → 7 → 11 → 18 → 29 → ?

D 1 → 2 → 3 → 5 → 11 → ?

Imagine you have a pan of milk and a pan of orange juice. First you take a cup of the orange juice and mix it with the milk. Then you take a cup of the milk-and-orange-juice mixture, and put it back into the pan of orange juice. Is there more orange juice in the milk or more milk in the orange juice?

Eight men are in a room. Each man shakes hands with each of the others. How many handshakes are there?

What is the weight of a fish that weighs ten pounds plus half its weight?

Suppose you keep your socks in a drawer that is the fourth from the top and the third from the bottom. How many drawers are there in the chest?

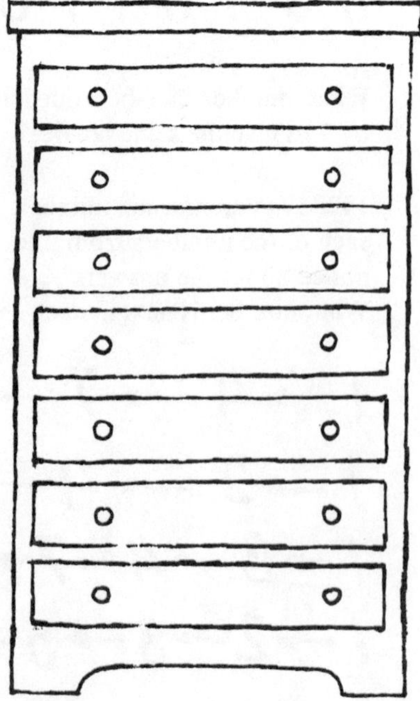

These fifteen links are to be joined into one long chain. It costs one cent to cut a link and two cents to weld a link together. What would be the cheapest way to make the chain?

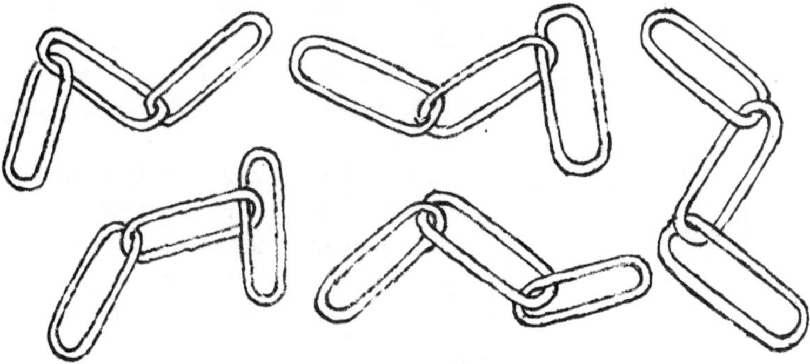

Suppose one million nickels were placed side by side in a long line. How many miles long would the line be?

How can you figure out the weight of one page in a telephone book?

Figure out how fast you can run. Measure off 100 feet and time how many seconds it takes for you to run this distance. Then compute your speed in miles per hour. Can you run faster than twelve miles per hour?

What time is it?

How many times in twelve hours does the minute hand of a clock pass the hour hand?
How much time passes between the time the minute hand and the hour hand on a clock meet, then meet again?
If it takes 5 seconds for a clock to strike five o'clock, how long will it take for the clock to strike ten o'clock?
There is a power blackout at five-thirty in the afternoon. The next morning you notice that an electric clock says three-thirty when it is eleven by your wrist watch. How long was the electricity off, and when did it go back on?

14 funny trees

What could have caused this pine tree to grow in a loop?

Crooked trees

How was the tree trunk bent so high up? Was the bend made closer to the ground when the tree was smaller?

What made the tree grow crooked?

. . . Electricity in the wires killed the center of the tree.

. . . There is more light to the left.

. . . A car hit the tree when it was smaller.

. . . The power company had the tree's top cut off to keep it from hitting the wires.

Why are all the branches growing out from only one side of this pine tree?

What caused the tree to grow in this unusual shape?

What made these two trees grow together?

Why are the roots of the large oak tree sticking out of the ground?

What happened to the inside of this tree trunk?

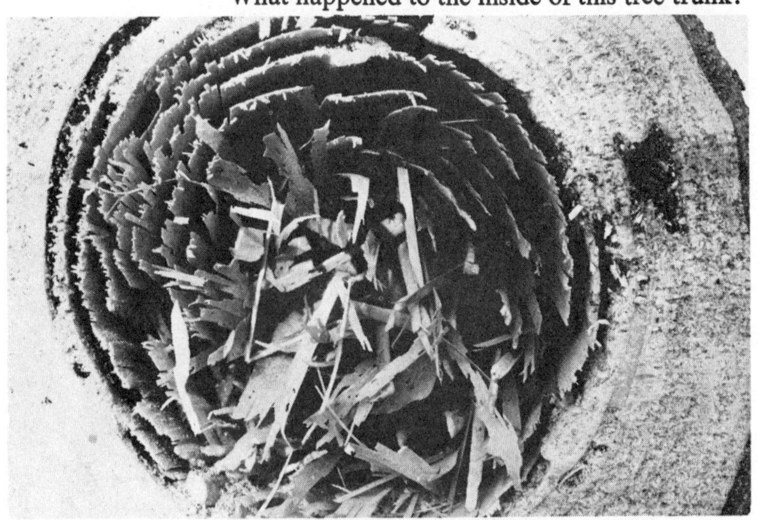

Why were the wires put through the tree?

96

Plants growing in funny places

How did the tree start growing high up on the chimney?

How did the plants get underneath the asphalt paving?

Did this tree grow faster when it was young or during its older years?

Make a polished tree slab

A good way to study tree rings is to prepare a shiny slice of wood. Saw a slab about one inch thick from a log or large fallen branch. A few days should be allowed for drying if the wood is green or wet. One side of the dried slab should be smoothed with sand paper and then rubbed with linseed oil. Try to make several slabs from different pieces of wood.

Look at the rings on the polished surfaces. Can you tell the age of the trees? Are all the rings the same width? Do some trees grow faster than others?

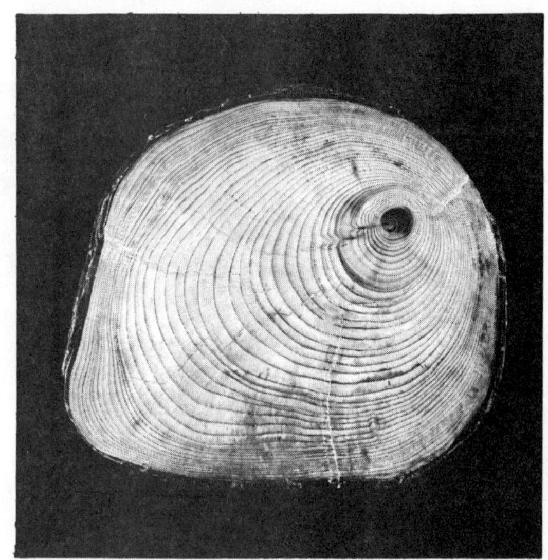

What might have happened to this tree to cause the off-center rings?

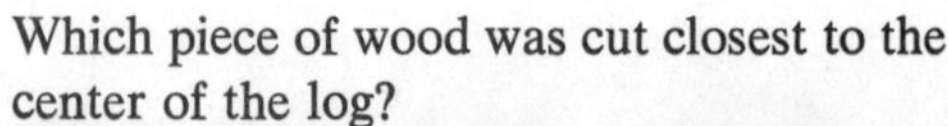

Which piece of wood was cut closest to the center of the log?

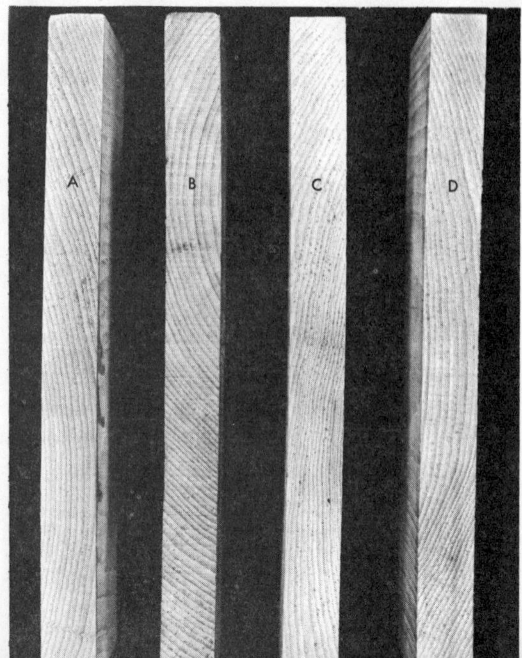

15 bulbs and batteries

The two wires from the batteries are bare of insulation where they connect with the bulb underwater. Why doesn't the electricity "short circuit" through the water instead of lighting the bulb?

A small hole was punched in the base of this light bulb while it was underwater. Why did most of the bulb fill with water? What is in the small bubble at the top of the bulb?

How would you connect the bell, battery, and switches so that the bell will ring when *either* switch is closed?

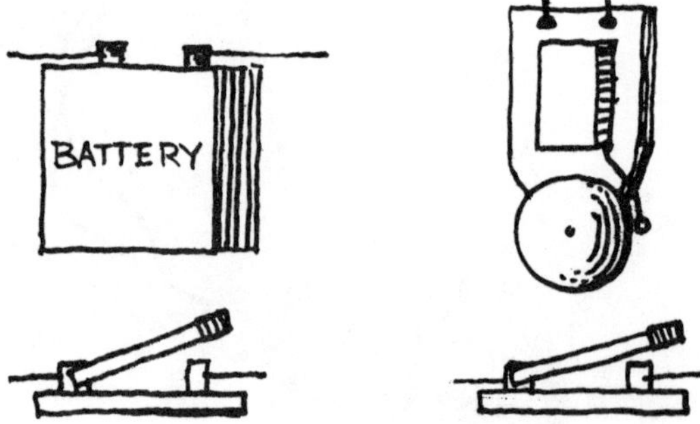

Where would wires be attached so that one switch will light the bulb, and the other switch will ring the bell?

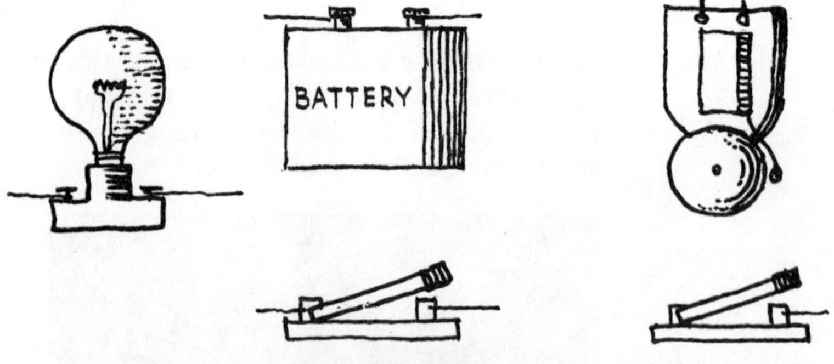

What will happen when the switch is closed?

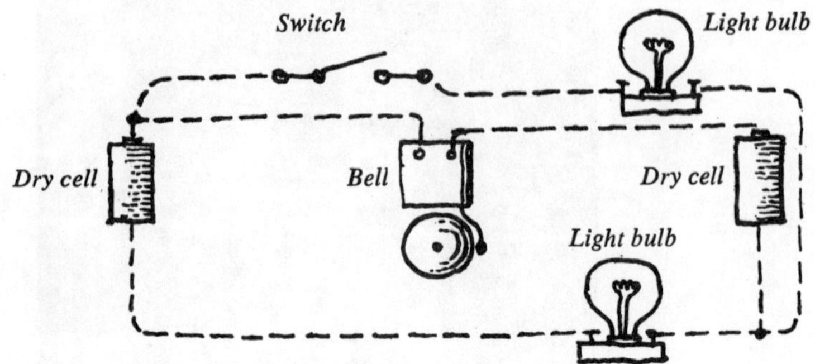

Which battery will last longest?

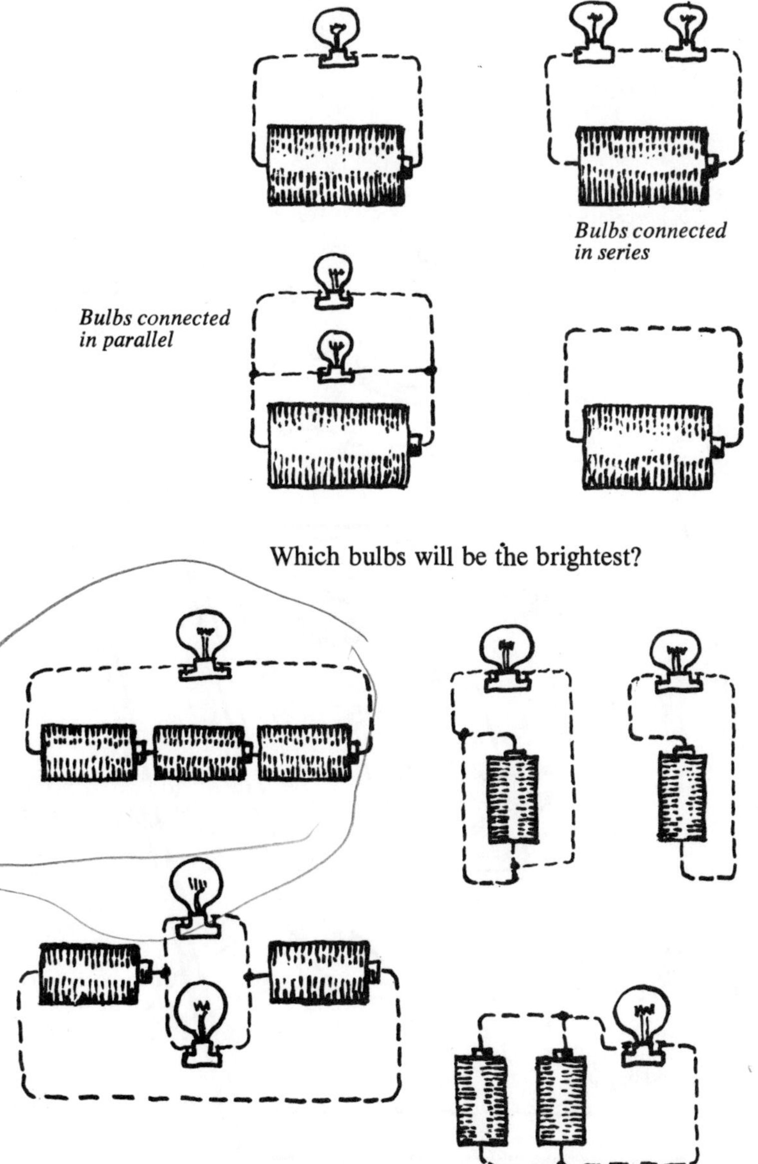

Which bulbs will be the brightest?

102

Make a penny-pitching game

Can you see why the bulb lights when the penny lands between the two aluminum foil strips?

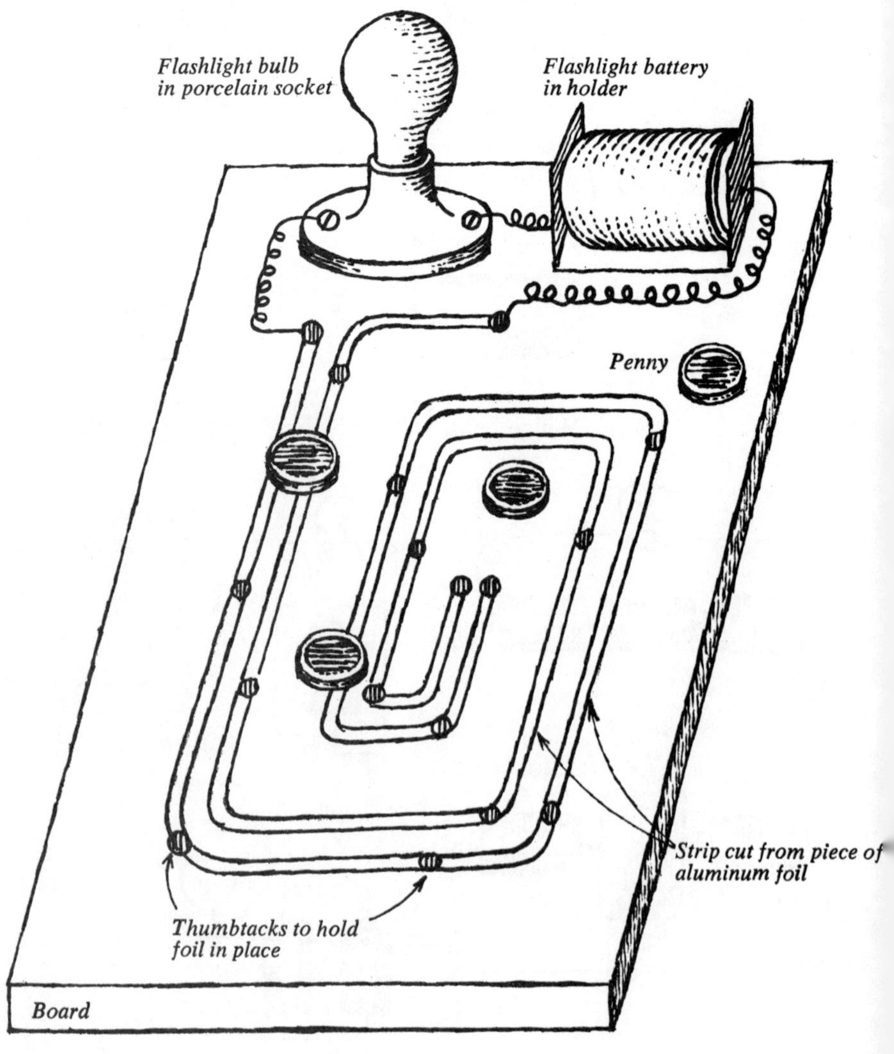

Make a rain alarm

When water falls, it dissolves the lump of sugar. Then the jaws of the spring clothespin can come together and make contact. What else could be used in place of the sugar cube?

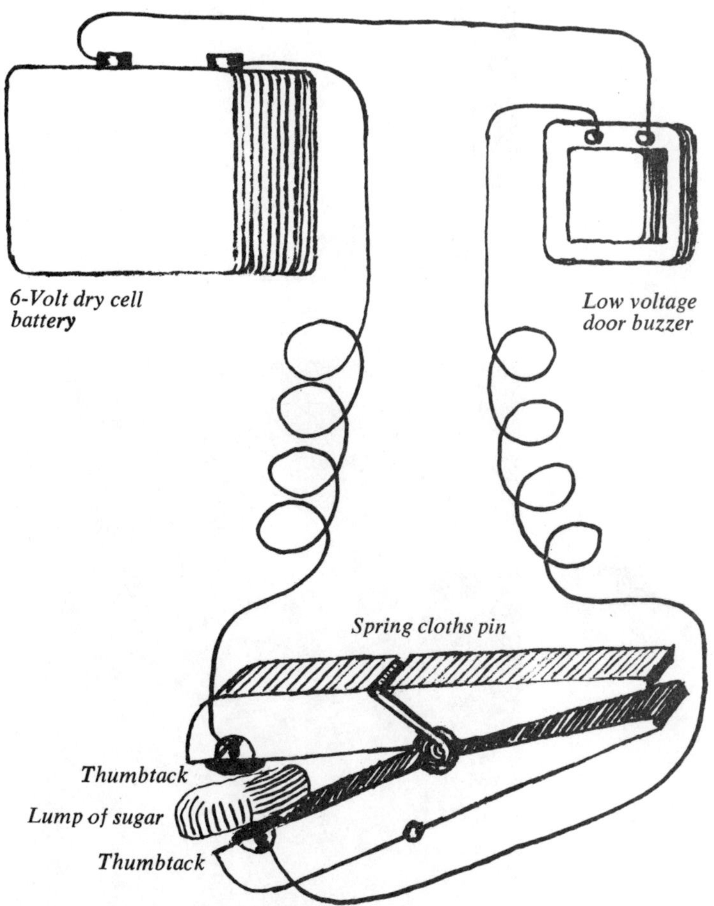

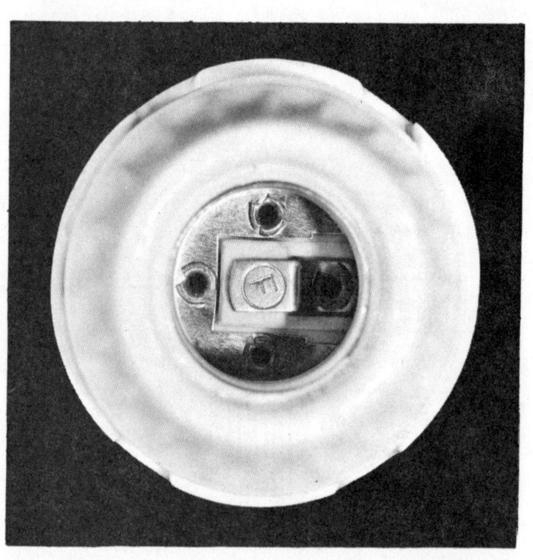

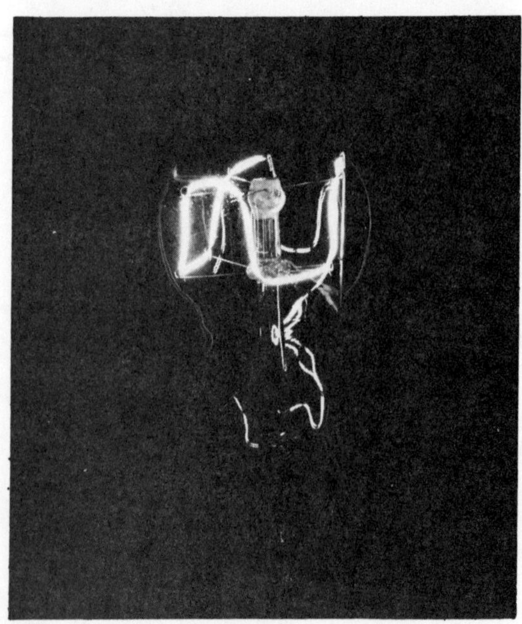

16 what will happen if?

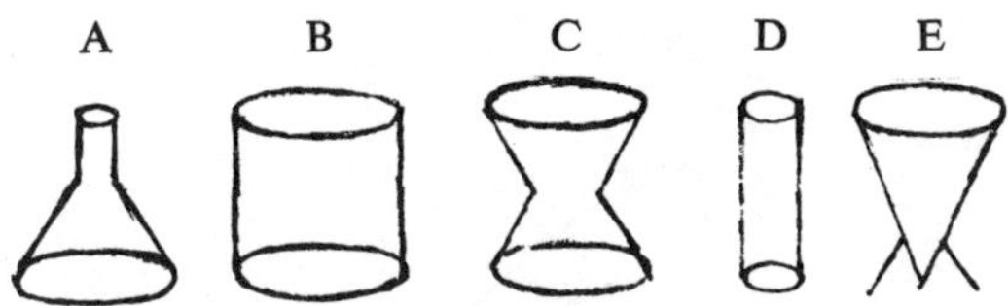

Suppose these five bottles were set outside to measure rainfall. Which bottle would collect the smallest amount of rain? Which would fill up first?

What will happen to a ball's bounce when it is cold? Drop a rubber ball from a table top and measure the height of its first bounce with a yardstick. Then cool the ball for an hour in your refrigerator. Will the cold ball bounce as high as it did before?

What will happen if you mount a candle as shown and then light it at both ends. Will the candle stay tilted the same way as it burns?

Straightened paper clip pushed through candle slightly above center line

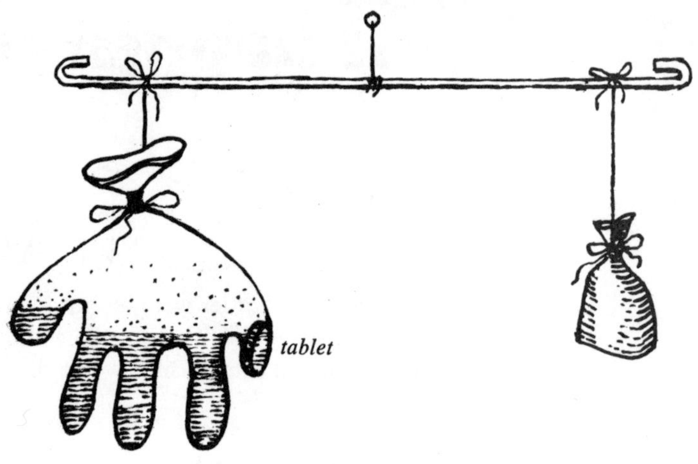

When the water is mixed with an Alka-Seltzer tablet, the plastic glove will fill up with carbon dioxide. When this happens, will the scale still balance?

Suppose a piece of bread and an apple are sealed in a jar that is wet inside. The jar is then balanced on a scale and left for a month. As the food becomes moldy and decays, will the jar get lighter, stay almost the same, or stay exactly the same weight?

What will happen to the weight of popcorn after popping? Will it weigh more, less, or the same? Why?

Make a pair of coupled pendulums with string and two small weights. Loop the string over a straw, as shown in the diagram. Then start one pendulum moving by pulling the weight out to the side. Watch for a while to see what happens. Move the straw up higher on the two strings and start one of the pendulums swinging again. What difference do you notice? Try the straw lower down, also.

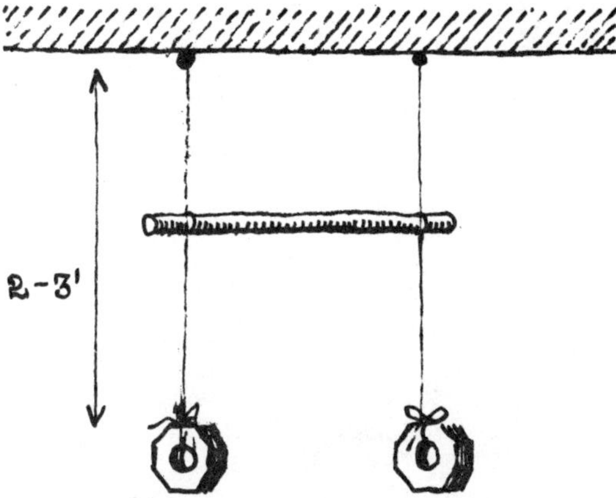

Hang two weights on strings and start them swinging around one another. How long will the weights keep winding up and unwinding?

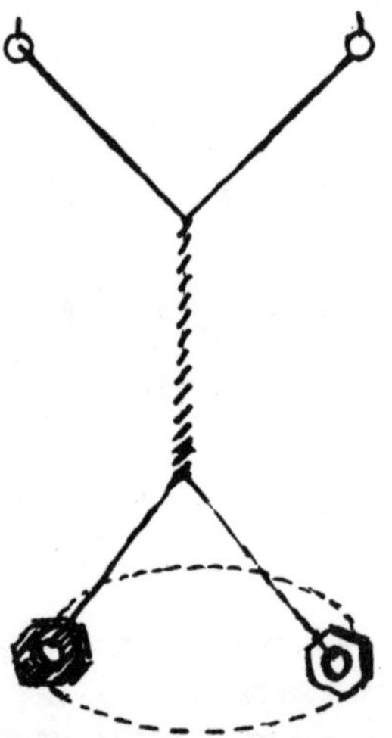

Next, change one of the weights so it is heavier than the other one. Do the weights still wind and unwind the same way?

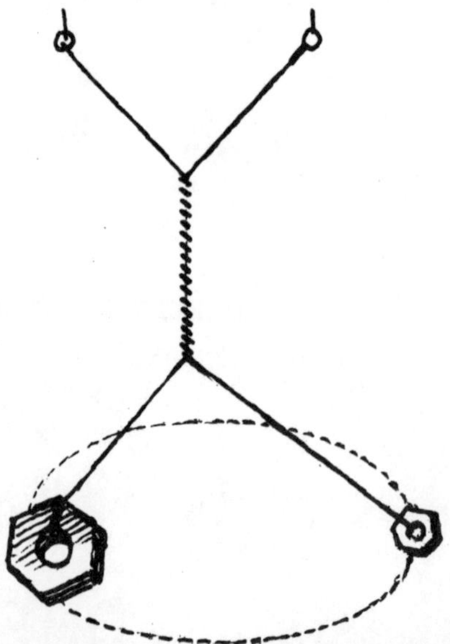

Cut up a piece of paper into a lot of strips that are about ¾ of an inch wide and 8 inches long. Then cut them in the shapes shown. Where do you think each paper strip will break when you pull on both ends of it with your hands? Before pulling, use a pencil to mark the place where you think the strip will rip. If you can't break some of the strips, have someone else pull on one end.

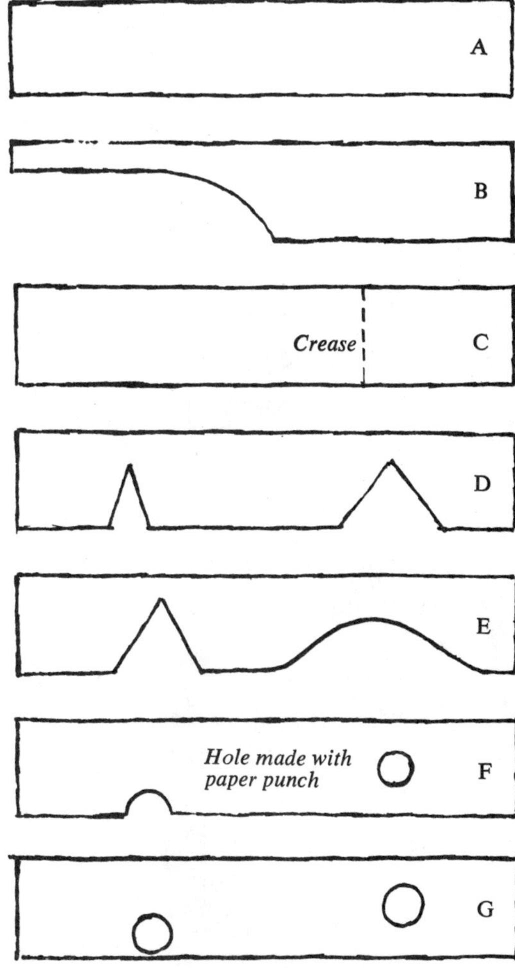

Cut small pieces of aluminum foil into the three shapes shown here. Then put drops of wax on the ends of each strip. Attach Scotch tape handles and heat each strip at the center, as shown. Can you guess which end of each strip will heat up faster, and melt the wax?

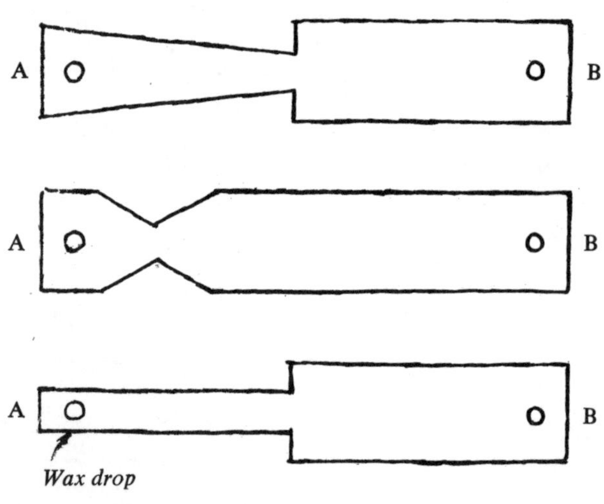

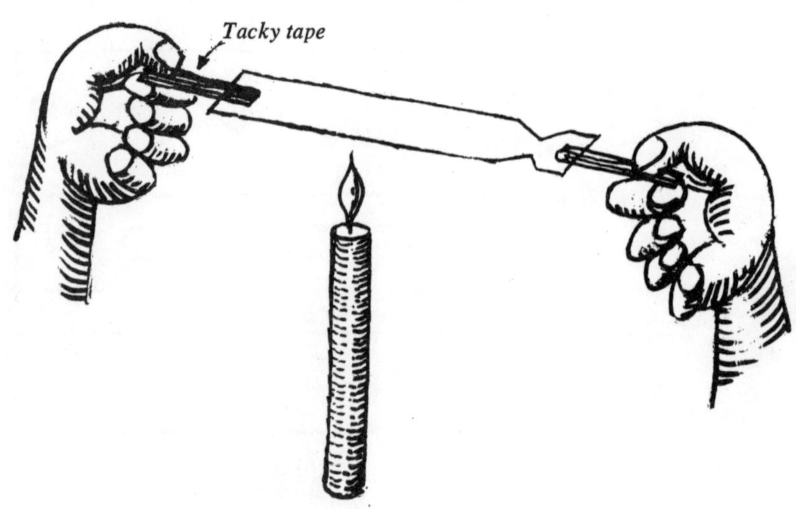

17 experiments on you

How strong are you?

Can you break a round toothpick held between three fingers, as shown? You can't use your other hand or anything else.

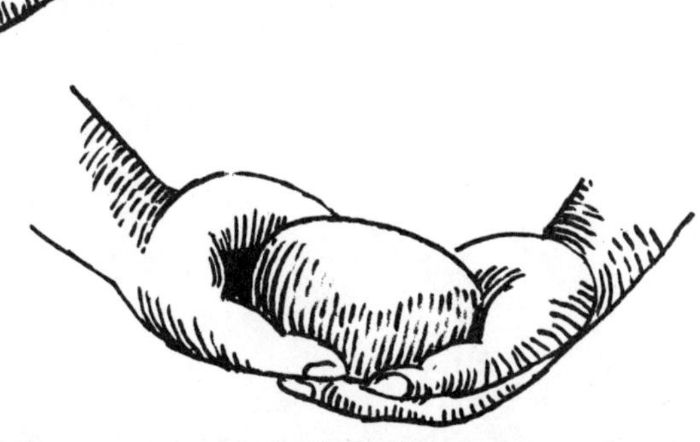

Place a raw egg lengthwise between your hands. Can you break the egg by squeezing your hands together?

Can you pick up a chair by lifting at the bottom of a leg with just one hand?

Measuring the strength of your finger muscles

How strong are your muscles? You can test the strength of your finger muscles by challenging a friend to a finger-pulling contest. Interlock forefingers and pull. The winner is the one who can force the other's finger to uncurl and let go. Another game you can play is thumb wrestling. Grasp hands with an opponent and then attempt to pin his thumb beneath your own thumb.

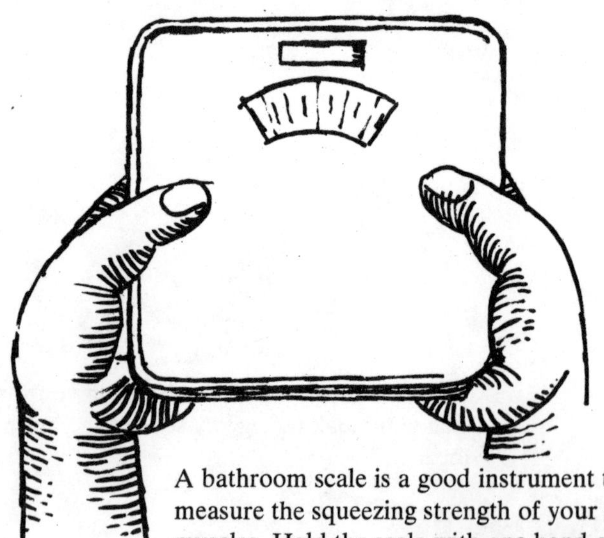

A bathroom scale is a good instrument to measure the squeezing strength of your finger muscles. Hold the scale with one hand on either side and squeeze as hard as you can. Can you make the scale read more than 60 pounds? Let your friends try, too. Are heavier people always stronger than lighter people?

Muscles becomes temporarily weaker if they are used continually. To see how much strength your finger muscles lose, open and close your fingers as fast and as hard as you can for a minute. Then immediately squeeze the scale again. Are your fingers less than half as strong? How long does it take for the muscles to regain their original strength?

Can you do it?

Can you touch something with your right hand that you can't touch with your left hand?
Can you catch a baseball without moving your hands backward?
Can you write the number 6 while moving your right leg in a circular clockwise path?
Can you inhale through your nose while exhaling through your mouth?
Can you eat a meal by moving your jaw only up and down rather than chewing from side to side?
Can you swallow some water when a teaspoon is in your mouth?

Can you swallow water while you are upside down?

114
Tricks with your eyes

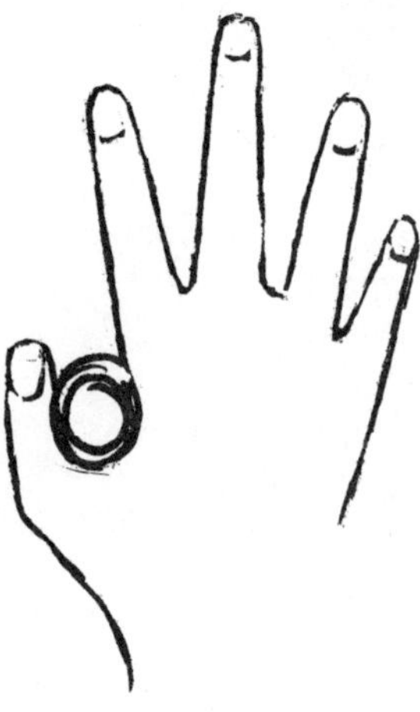

Roll up a piece of paper into a paper tube about one inch in diameter. Hold the tube between the thumb and forefinger of your right hand. With both eyes open, look through the tube with your left eye. Does your hand appear to have a hole through it?

Make a pinhole in a small piece of paper. Hold the paper about an inch from your eye, and look through the hole. At the same time, hold a pin by the point with your other hand so that the pinhead is between the hole and your eye. If you move the pin up, it should look as though it is coming down from the top. Which way does the pin seem to go when it is moved from left to right?

Hold a toothpick in each hand, and try to touch them together while one eye is closed.

Can you see at all when it is completely dark? Even in the woods on a dark, stormy night there is some light. To see what it is like without any light, turn out all the lights in your house after dark. Then go into a closet and shut the door. Can you see anything? Open and close your eyes to see if there is any difference.

What would happen if your ears were where your eyes are?

In this optical illusion, a series of complete circles appear to make a spiral.

For science experts only

When you put your hand under cool running water from a faucet, the water feels cold. But when you drink this same water, it feels much warmer. How can this be?

If you wear a ring, notice how loose it is on your finger at bedtime, and then see how much tighter it is when you wake in the morning. Why does the ring seem to tighten up during the night?

Veins in your body appear blue through the skin because the blood in them is bluish. When you cut a vein, however, the blood comes out red. Why?

Hold one hand down and the other hand over your head for fifteen seconds. Then put your hands together so you can see their color. Why is one hand redder than the other one?

Why does it hurt when you drink ginger ale or soda too fast?

How large is your body?

You can measure your volume in a bathtub. Fill it about half full and mark the level of the water with crayon on the side of the tub. Now jump in and try to get all the way underwater. When the water becomes still, have someone mark the new height. Step out and pour in quarts or gallons of water until the level again reaches the second line. What is your volume in pints? Can you calculate your density in pounds per pint?

How fast do your fingernails grow?

Do you know how fast your fingernail grows? You can find out by scratching a line on your nail at the cuticle. Use a fingernail file or a triangular metal file. See how long it takes for the mark to move a quarter of an inch from the cuticle. You could try marking a toenail, too.

How fast does your hair grow?

How can you figure out a way to measure how long it takes your hair to grow an inch?

Be a fingerprint detective

Every time you touch something smooth with a finger, you leave a *latent,* or nearly invisible, fingerprint. Get some latent prints by holding a clean drinking glass between your fingers. You can make the prints easier to see with talcum powder. Shake a little powder on the glass and then blow the powder off. Some powder should stick in the oil left by your fingers. "Lift" talcum powder prints with Scotch tape. Press a piece of tape on the print and then pull it off the glass. Study the print by sticking the tape on a piece of dark paper.

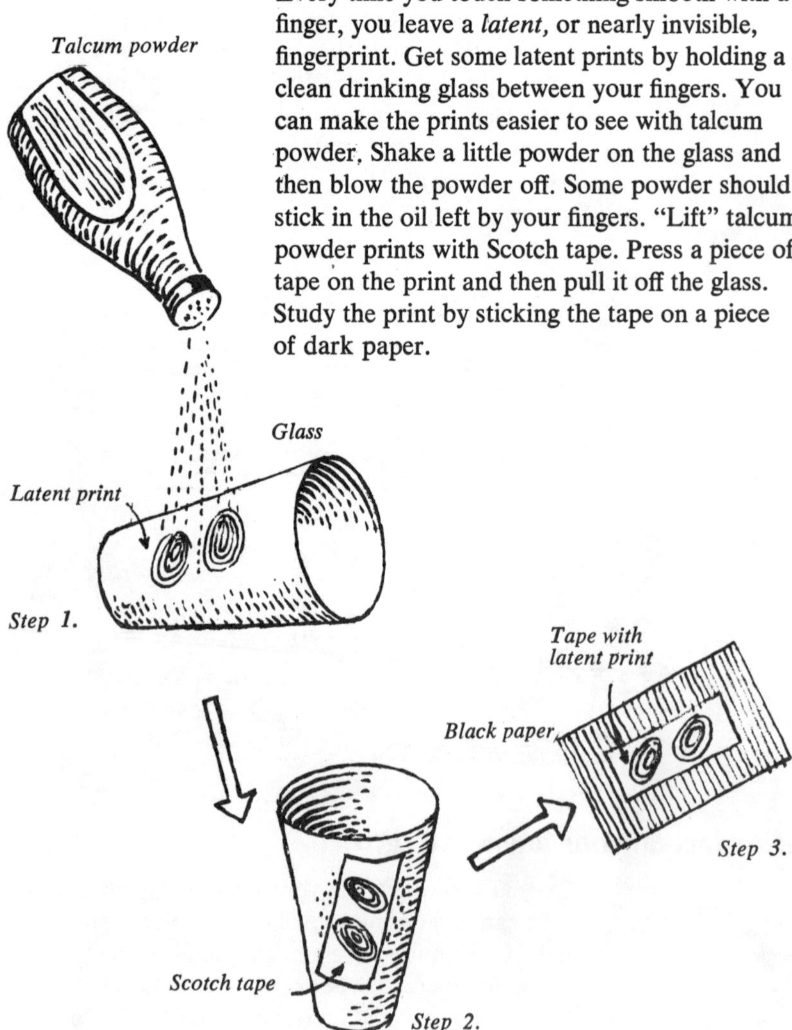

HOW TO LIFT LATENT PRINTS

18 just for fun

Make an ocean

Get a large jar, and fill it about two-thirds of the way with turpentine. Then fill the final third with rubbing alcohol. Add a few drops of blue food coloring, and screw on the top tightly. Turn the jar on its side, and slowly lift one end up and down. Can you make any waves?

Top patterns

Here is how you can make interesting patterns with a toy top. Place a piece of carbon paper on a table with the carbon side up, and put a sheet of white paper on top. Then spin the top so it moves around on the paper. After doing this several times, look at the underside of the paper.

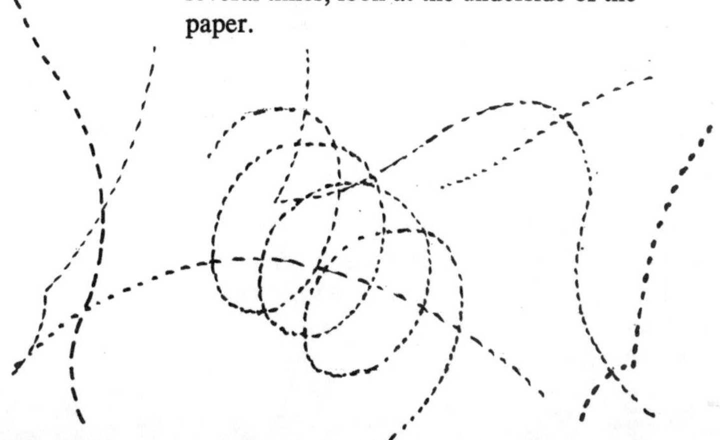

120
Can you pass the Idiot Test?

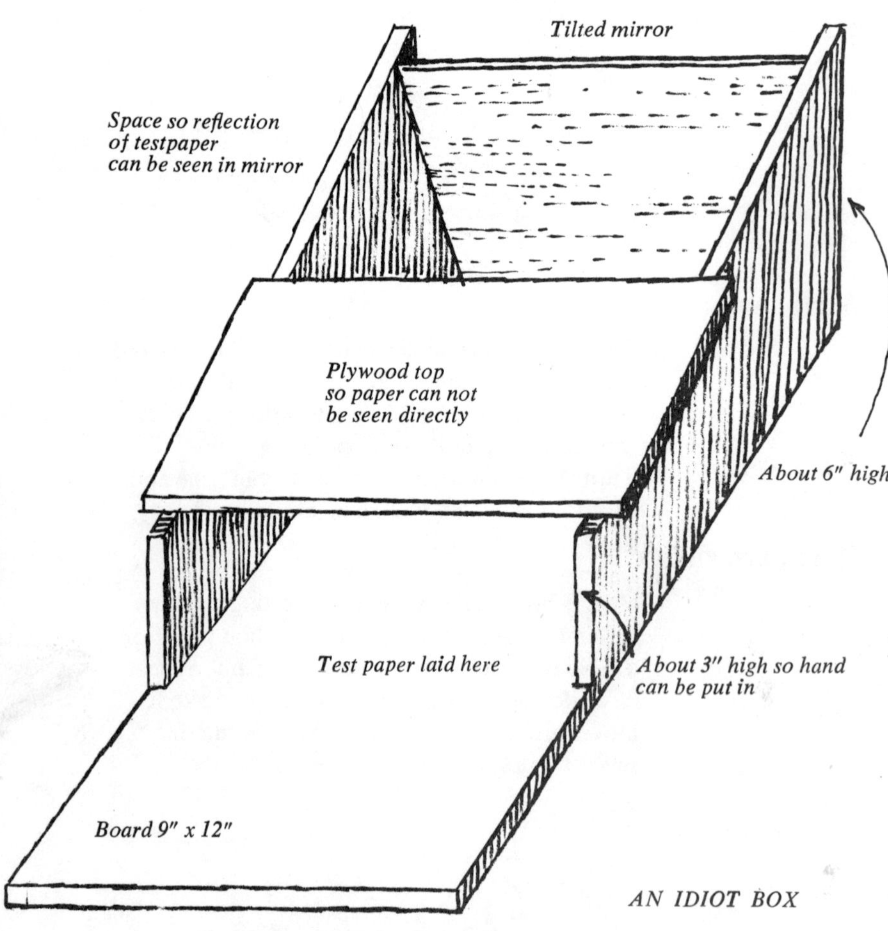

AN IDIOT BOX

To take the Idiot Test, you must follow a path with a pencil while looking in a mirror. The drawing shows how to make an Idiot Box. The mirror and top should be positioned so you can see the test paper only in the mirror.

Draw a curved path on a sheet of paper and see how well you can trace it in the Idiot Box. Let your friends try, too.

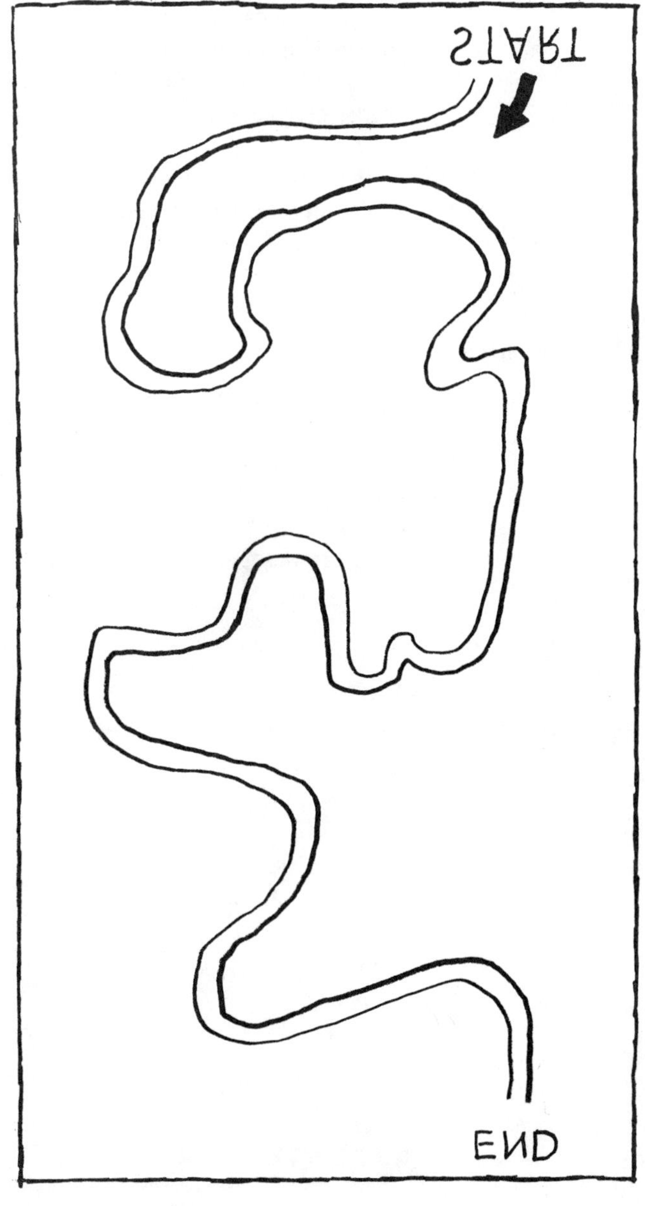

Junk sculpture

Try to get some old appliances and small machines to take apart. You should be able to find some of these things: a TV set, an old phonograph, a carburetor or generator from an automobile, a burned-out toaster, and an alarm clock. Take apart your used appliances with a screwdriver, pliers, an adjustable wrench, and a hammer.

Now the different parts can be reassembled into a junk sculpture. Fasten things together with wire or glue. Decorate your creation with spray paint.

Make a clock

One way the ancients kept track of time was with dripping water. If a pinhole is made in the bottom of a gallon plastic jug, water will drip out at a fairly regular rate.

Can you invent other gadgets that can be used to measure time?

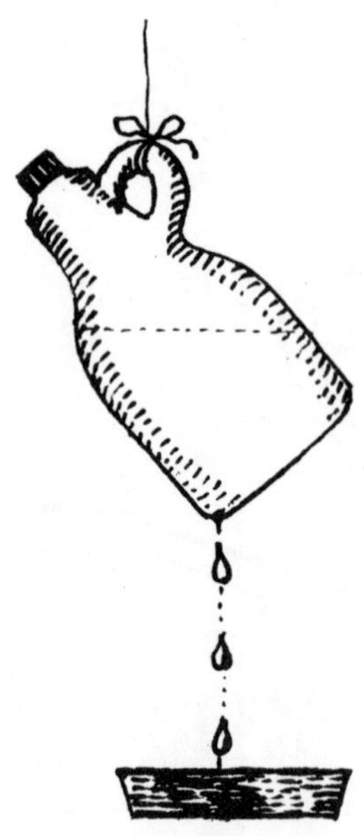

Trapping wild insects

Many kinds of insects can be captured in simple traps. Three different kinds are shown here. Crawling beetles and other ground bugs are unable to climb out of the tin can when they fall in. At night, moths are attracted to the molasses mixture and get stuck. When flying night insects enter the light trap, they usually are unable to find their way out.

How many different kinds of insects can you trap?

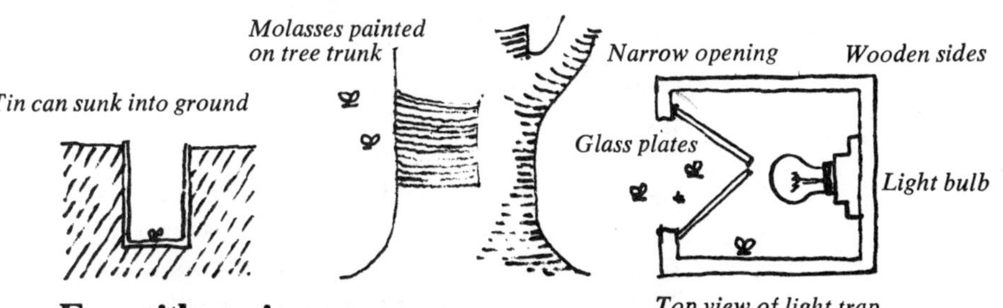

Top view of light trap

Fun with a microscope

It is easy to watch salt crystals grow when looking through a microscope. Keep stirring salt into water until no more will dissolve. Then place a drop on a microscope slide and with a microscope watch it dry up. You should see salt crystals form as the drop becomes smaller and smaller.

Another way to see crystals form is with Crystal Glaze. This liquid is sold in some art stores for decorating glass. Paint some on a microscope slide and watch it through the microscope. The liquid will begin to dry immediately and form beautiful crystals. A microscope magnifies motion just as it does size. Look through a hand lens at the minute hand of a watch. Does it seem to be moving fast? Lay a wall thermometer under your microscope so you can see the top of the red liquid inside the tube. Blow on the thermometer and see if the liquid moves.

Fun with eggs

Place an uncooked egg on a plate and spin it around as fast as you can. While it is still spinning, stop it for an instant with your finger. If the egg is let go immediately, it will start to spin again. This is because the insides of the egg keep turning for a few seconds after the shell is stopped.

Put an uncooked egg in the kitchen sink and let the water from the faucet run on it. The egg should stay under the stream of water by itself. What other objects will stay under the faucet and what things get pushed aside by the water?

You can get the insides out of an egg by poking a small hole in each end with a pin. Then blow hard into one hole, and the egg should come out the hole in the other end. For fun, refill the eggshell with water and seal the holes with tape or melted wax. Then smash it over the head of a friend. He will think you have hit him with a real egg.

Some science tricks

Put a little pile of salt in the center of the bottom of a drinking glass and spin the glass. The salt will be spread around the sides of the glass. Then put some water into the glass with the salt and stir the water around with a spoon. Now the salt goes to the center.

Have your mother or father help you with this one. Light a candle and leave the match burning. Blow out the candle. While the candle is still smoking, hold the lighted match in the smoke above the candlewick. You should see the flame from the match jump down the smoke and relight the candle.

Lay a yardstick or thin strip of wood on a table so about half of it is sticking over the edge. Then smooth out several sheets of newspaper over the part of the stick on the table. Hit the end of the stick as hard as you can with the side of your hand. The stick should snap in half.

Which brand of paper towels is best?

You can experiment to find out which kind of paper towels are most absorbent or have the greatest strength. At a supermarket, buy rolls of towels made by three different companies.

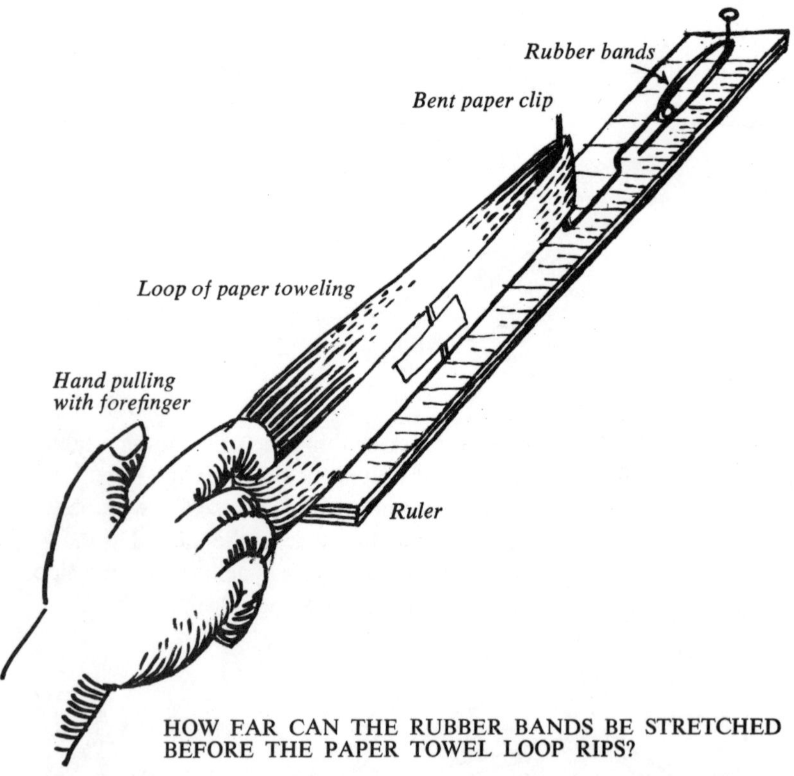

HOW FAR CAN THE RUBBER BANDS BE STRETCHED BEFORE THE PAPER TOWEL LOOP RIPS?

To check water absorption, squeeze a "soaking wet" towel into a glass so you can measure how much water it held. Another way to measure absorption is to drip water on a towel held over a table. How many drops does it take before the water penetrates the towel and drips through? It is more difficult to devise methods for measuring paper strength. See if you can invent some.

An easy way to print photographs

Photo stores sell studio proof paper that you can use to print pictures. Place a negative against the shiny side of the proof paper and hold it in the sun a few minutes until the paper is dark red. Bring the proof paper inside before you lift the negative to look at your picture. To make the print permanent, dip it into a hypo solution for a few seconds and wash with water.

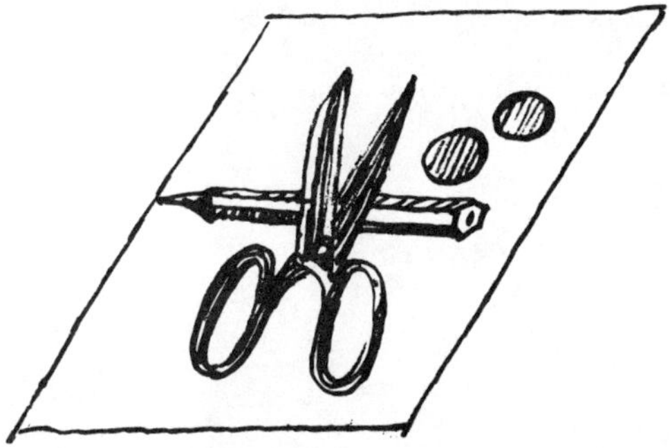

1. Place objects on studio proof paper and leave in sun a minute

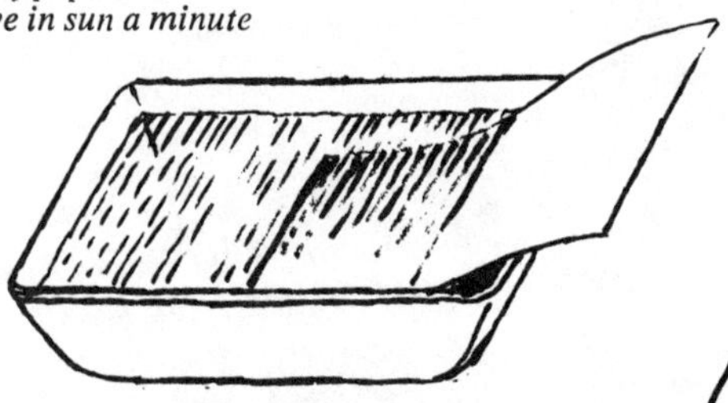

2. Soak paper in hypo (fixer) for a minute

3. Wash with water for a minute and dry in air

answers

Shadows

page 1

If a stick is pointed directly at the sun, no shadow can be seen.

The matchbox shadow with the sharper edges and even shading was made by light from the sun. Why does the shadow made in light from a bulb have such fuzzy edges?

page 2

Noon on Arpil 14—Shadow B
10:00 A.M. on June 14—Shadow A
10:00 A.M. on October 14—Shadow C

page 4

The photograph of the ocean was taken in New Jersey. If you were facing the ocean, the shadows would be going to your left. Since the noontime sun never is in the northern part of the sky in the United States, the ocean must be toward the east. In Australia, would you see noontime shadows like this in Sydney or in Perth?

The sun's shadow is not always shortest at noon. If you live near the eastern border of a time zone, the sun is highest in the sky before noon; in the western part of a time zone, the sun is highest sometime between noon and 12:30 P.M.

The interesting shadow of a soap bubble is dark around the edge and mottled inside.

A shadow can be smaller than the object that makes it. Almost all shadows cast by objects in the noontime sun are smaller.

page 5

The sketch shows an object made of modeling clay that would cast shadows similar to those illustrated on page 5.

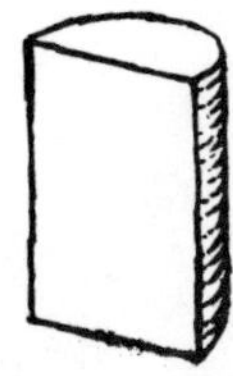

To make a square shadow with a postcard, hold the card in sunlight and tip up one end.

Here is how to make a round light spot with a square hole. Fold a sheet of paper in half and cut a *very tiny* triangle out of the folded edge. When you open the paper you will have a square hole. Hold the paper in the sunlight and allow the light to fall on another piece of paper about a foot away. You should see a circular spot of light: the image of the round sun.

If a pencil is held between two indoor lights, two shadows will be formed. What happens as the pencil is moved toward one of the lights?

page 6

The shadow is from a picket fence and gate.

page 7

Top: Tree trunks
Bottom: Large bridge

page 8

Craters are easiest to see in the area of the moon where night meets day. Here the ridges are lighted, but the crater bottoms are shaded. What do the shadows indicate about the craters' depths?

The sun is millions of miles away—off the top of the photo.

Unless it is in an eclipse, half of the moon's surface is always in darkness.

Mystery photos

page 9

The patterns on the wall were left when the building that once adjoined it was torn down. The diagonal lines show where the stairs were.

page 10

The photo is an upside-down view of a chain-link fence that is covered with snow. Turn it right side up, and you can see trees through the open spaces in the fence.

page 11

Top: The photograph shows the inside of an eighteenth-century observation tower. The sunlight coming in each window on the right side shines below each opposite window on the left side. This means that the picture must have been taken looking up.
Bottom: The picture of two squash courts has been tipped on its right side.

page 12

Top: Broken asphalt paving
Bottom: Air bubbles under ice on lake

page 13

Top: Moss
Bottom: Cracks in dried mud

page 14

Top: Ice on chain-link fence
Bottom: Dried mud flakes

page 15

Top: The rack is used to toast four slices of bread on a gas stove burner.
Bottom: The glove is to protect the fingers when shooting a bow.

page 16

Top: The wasp nest is square because it was made inside the wall of an old house

Bottom: Sea gulls cannot stand on water. The birds in the photograph are on smooth ice.

page 17

Top: The sand dunes were formed when a wind was blowing from the left. The sand piles up steeper on the windward side of a dune.
Bottom: The holes in the tree were made by a pileated woodpecker.

page 18

Top: A sign painted on the road is usually viewed from a slant by the driver in a car. Hold the picture at a slant, and the letters should look normal.
Bottom: Snow piles along the road often contain the remains of salt that was used to melt ice. As the snow melts, salty melt water flows away from the snow. When the water evaporates, the salt is left behind in a white line.

Drops and bubbles

page 19

Water thrown into the air makes drops of many sizes.

As water flows faster from a faucet, a twisting, unbroken column of water is formed.

Water drops in a hot frying pan roll around on a layer of steam.

A water drop in oil takes an almost spherical shape.

Lead shot is made by pouring molten lead through a screen at the top of a shot tower. As it falls, the lead forms liquid drops which are hardened in a water bath at the bottom.

page 20

Water drops on wax paper are not all the same size and shape.

The drawing is wrong because it shows large water drops that are almost spherical. Large drops on wax paper are actually somewhat flattened.

Surface tension creates an elastic "skin" covering the outside of a water drop. The skin also clings to a pencil point and pulls the rest of the drop along.

It is quite difficult to make a drop smaller than a pinhead. Try shaking your wet hands high above wax paper. Some of the water drops will break as they strike the paper and make much smaller drops.

Since soap destroys most of the surface tension, a drop touched with soap becomes much flatter.

Small drops magnify more than large drops because smaller drops are more spherical.

Large drops usually roll down a tipped paper before small drops do.

page 21

Top: A wide stream of water takes longer to break into drops than a narrow column.
Bottom: The photograph shows dew on the hood of a 1964 Pontiac.

page 22

A drop of water weighs about 1/400 of an ounce.

Surface tension squeezes a drop into a shape that has the least surface area: a sphere.

The earth was once an enormous molten sphere.

A bubble is a hollow drop.

Small bubbles in syrup are spherical. Large bubbles rise faster than smaller ones. All bubbles eventually float to the surface of the syrup.

page 24

The size of individual bubbles in a raft can be varied by blowing harder and softer, and by using a large straw.

page 25

On a very cold day, soap bubbles shatter before they freeze.

To push your finger inside a bubble, first wet your fingers with liquid soap.

To blow one bubble inside another, place a large bubble on a wet surface. Then wet a drinking straw in the bubble liquid and push the straw into the bubble. Now see if you can blow another bubble inside the first bubble.

Balloons

page 26

It requires a lot of effort to hold a balloon underwater.

If a balloon is only partly blown up, it might stay in one piece when popped. Also, a balloon filled with water should break in one piece.

page 27

To blow up a balloon inside a bottle, first heat the air in the bottle by running hot water over it for a minute. Quickly push the balloon into the bottle and stretch the balloon's mouth over the top of the bottle. Then place it in the refrigerator. As the air cools and contracts, the balloon will blow up inside the bottle.

Here is how you might be able to blow up one balloon inside of another. Put one balloon inside another, and blow them both up a little. Then tie off the inner balloon. Continue blowing up the outside balloon.

page 28

A large balloon falls more slowly than a small balloon. As the balloon falls, it is slowed down by the air that it must push aside. Because a large balloon meets more air resistance, it drops slower than a smaller balloon.

The balloon tends to be attracted to a stream of water.

page 29

A charged balloon loses its charge of electricity to the air and the ceiling. Since this usually occurs within several hours, a balloon could never stay on the ceiling for a week.
Two charged balloons will repel one another.
A narrow stream of water is bent toward a charged balloon.

None of the methods suggested is very effective in preventing a balloon from slowly collapsing.

page 30

The water from a pinhole in a water balloon at first squirts farther as the balloon gets larger. When the rubber stretches more, however, the pinhole becomes larger and the stream of water decreases in length. What will happen to the stream from the pinhole as water is released from the balloon through its mouth?

page 31

On an unlevel surface, an air puck moves toward the lowest edge. The speed of a puck increases as it slides down an incline. When two pucks collide, they bounce off one another and continue to move.

page 32

A pinprick causes the balloon rubber to rip.

As a car slows down, the air and everything else inside it that is not fastened to the car keeps moving forward. The air piles up in front of the lighter helium-filled balloon, pushing it backward.

When it rained, raindrops collected on the helium balloon. The weight of the water made the balloon fall to the ground.

Can you do it?

page 33

One way to drink with two straws is to block off the open straw with a finger.

It is difficult to drink water through fifteen straws because air leaks into your mouth between some of the straws.

It is possible to drink through a straw that has a pinhole in the middle, but the water is full of air bubbles when it gets to your mouth.

If no air can get into a soda bottle filled with water, you will be unable to suck out much water through a straw. What will happen if you blow into the straw?

page 34

To make a hunk of clay float, mold it in the shape of a small bowl. How much weight can you put into the clay boat before it sinks?

To make the loop of thread circular, place a drop of soap on top of the water enclosed by the thread. The loop should immediately become round.

It is not possible to fold a piece of paper in half nine times, regardless of its size or thinness.

To throw a ball and make it come back without hitting something, throw it straight up into the air.

To drop a coin so that it stays on its edge, you can make it spin. Hold the coin loosely between your thumb and forefinger a few inches above a table. Snap the edge of the coin with your other forefinger. It should drop to the table and spin on its edge for a few seconds.

After water soaks up a strip of newspaper more than three or four inches, it evaporates faster than more water can move up. To prevent this, enclose the newspaper strip in a wax-paper cover. Then the water should climb six inches or more.

page 36

Your friend can always see your face in a mirror if you can see his.

To see ten reflections, hold a hand mirror beside your eye. Then stand with your nose touching the bathroom mirror and adjust the small mirror until you can see a lot of eyes. Can you make even more reflections with three mirrors?

Freezing and melting ice

page 37

Top: The icicle was formed under the roof of the house, where the wire is attached. When the weather became warmer, the icicle broke away from the roof and slid down the wire.
Bottom: When a car's windshield wipers are used, tiny pieces of dirt are caught under the blades and scratch the windshield in curved lines. Dust then collects in the scratches while the wipers are not in use. The frost tends to form first around the dust particles in these scratches.

page 38

The jar that is filled with water and capped will probably be the only one to break when the water freezes. If the salt water has a lot of salt, it will only freeze into soft slush.

Ocean water will freeze, but not quite as solidly as plain water. It freezes at a temperature of 29° F. Large stretches of the sea in the Arctic and Antarctic are covered by thick layers of salt ice. Does salt ice taste like salt water?

Frozen milk does become hard, but never as firm as ice. When thawed out, it tastes almost like normal milk.

page 39

Ice freezes at 32° F., but gets as cold as the surrounding air. If your freezer is 10° F., the ice will eventually reach this temperature.

Here is how to make ice cubes of different colors. Color some water with food coloring and fill the bottom third of an ice tray with it. When the water is frozen, add a second layer of different-colored water and freeze the second layer. Then add a third color for freezing.

When the water is completely frozen, it is still possible to see the ice cube that was floating in it.

An ice cube forms first around the outside; the middle becomes ice last. Since water expands as it freezes, some ice is pushed up in the center of the cube. Why doesn't a frozen lake have a large bump in the middle, too?

Some solids such as ice, mothballs, and iodine crystals can slowly change into a gas without first going through the liquid stage. Ice can change into water vapor even at freezing temperatures.

The pan of oil happened to be placed under the edge of the garage roof where rain would run into it. Rain water is denser than oil, so the water sank to the bottom of the pan. As the pan filled with water, the oil floating on the water ran over the top of the pan and onto the ground. When winter came, the water froze.

page 40

The ice cube in cold water will melt first.

An ice cube will melt overnight in the refrigerator.

The melting of ice cubes outside depends upon the type of material on which they are placed, its color, and the location of the sun. Different materials vary in their capacity to absorb heat from the sun.

page 41

As the ice cube in cooking oil melts, the water stays on the bottom. Why doesn't the water float on the oil?

As an ice cube melts, it drips slower and slower. This is because a small piece of ice has a smaller surface area exposed to the warm air than a larger piece of ice.

The water from melted ice has the same weight as the ice itself. A tiny amount of water might evaporate before you looked at the scale again, but this change in weight would be too small to affect an ordinary scale.

Air from a fan would make an ice cube melt a lot faster. Air blowing from a fan is not really colder; it just feels that way. You could prove this with a thermometer. As an ice cube melts, the air around it becomes cooler. A fan blows more warm air by the ice, making it melt faster.

An icicle freezes as it melts.

page 42

Top: A snowplow dug up a piece of sod and left it buried in a snow pile. As the ice melted, the sod reached the surface and protected the snow beneath from the sun. Later the snow all around it melted faster, leaving the pillar of snow capped by the sod.
Bottom: The pilings absorb heat from the sun and melt the ice faster than the warm air.

Water

page 43

The sketch shows which globes and box sections contain water.

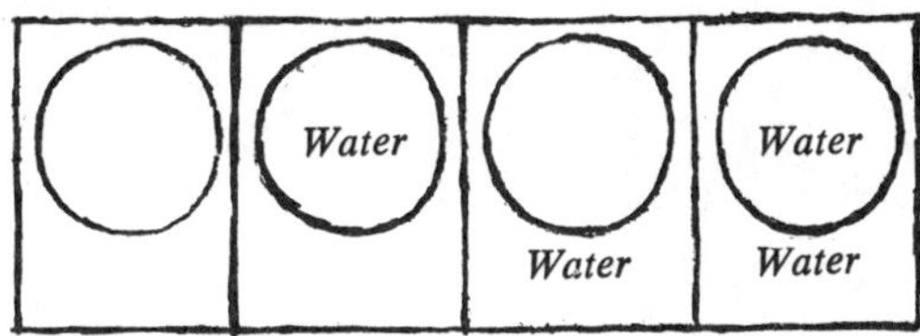

page 44

You can boil water in a paper cup because paper will not burn unless it gets a lot hotter than boiling water. The paper is kept cool by boiling water, and never gets hot enough to catch fire.

A wet spot on a chalkboard evaporates faster from the top because here the layer of water is thinnest. The spot changes size faster when it becomes smaller. Alcohol and gasoline evaporate faster than water.

You can prevent a drop of water from evaporating by placing it inside a tiny covered jar.

Fresh water evaporates quite a bit faster than salt water.

Most water contains a small amount of dissolved minerals. When water evaporates, the minerals are left behind in a thin layer. Try evaporating rain water, water from a stream, and tap water. Do you notice any difference in the amount of minerals deposited?

page 45

Water has condensed on the coolest portions of the watch crystal. Heat from the arm travels through the watch and warms the glass around the edge. Moisture has not collected in the very center because of heat coming from the post that holds the hands.

page 46

A piece of screen floats because of surface tension, the force that makes the surface of water act as if it were covered with an elastic skin. This force is not strong enough to prevent a stream of water from running through the screen.

Here is how the long wooden block would float. Would a square block made from four small blocks float this way also?

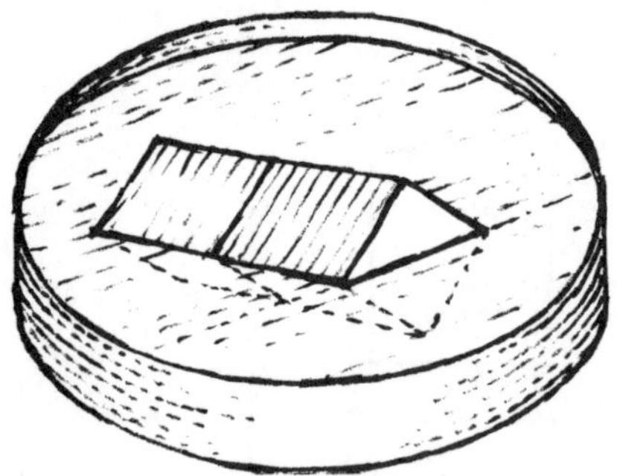

It is impossible to float a needle in soapy water. Soap weakens the surface tension of water so that it will not support a needle.

You can dissolve a drop of oil into a glass of water by adding a small amount of dishwashing soap. When the water is shaken, the oil will disappear.

page 47

Ice is less dense than water because it expands during freezing. The density of the oil is between that of ice and water.

Hot water will float for a while on top of cooler water. As the hot water cools, it sinks into the cold water and becomes mixed with it. When cold water is placed on top of hot water, the cold water sinks immediately.

page 48

Soda will come out the bottom hole in Can B and in Can C. Will soda come out either of the two holes in the bottom of Can D if it is tipped?

Water would squirt out fastest from the lowest hole (number 1). If this hole were closed, would water then come out the other holes faster?

If the milk carton with the four holes is held up, water will squirt farthest out of Hole 4. But if it is placed on the ground, the water coming from Hole 3 will shoot the greatest distance before hitting the ground.

page 49

When the valve is opened, water will flow out of the straight tube, and air will enter through the curved tube and bubble up through the water.

The sketches show where the water will be when the siphons stop.

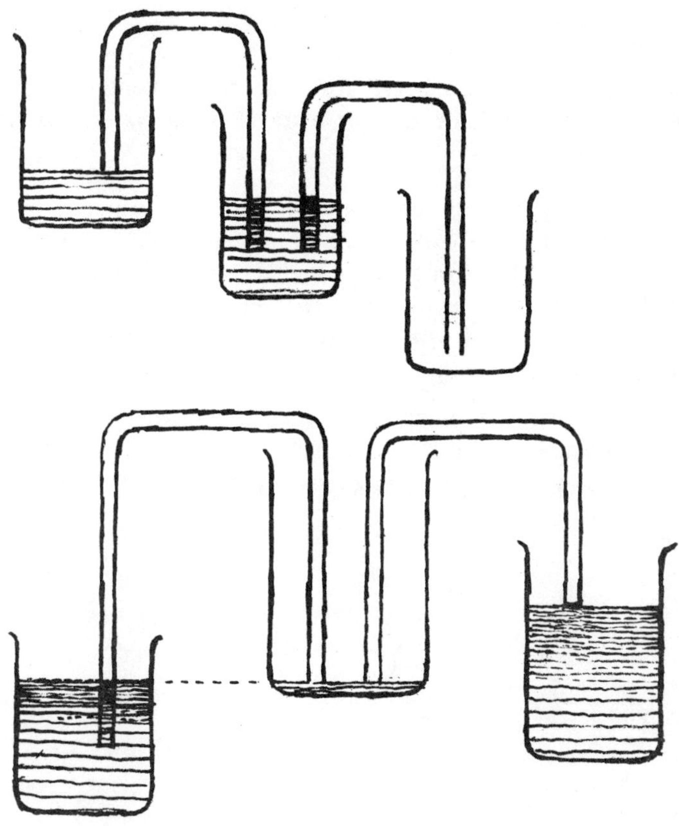

page 50

Water continues to travel up a blotter strip until it evaporates as fast as it rises. A narrow strip has a greater surface area relative to its size, and is thereby affected more by evaporation.

Water will rise up highest in the blotter strips and lowest in the writing paper. The bent blotter will act like a siphon, causing water to drip continuously from its bottom edge.

page 51

The water temperature in Glass A will be about 70° F. just after mixing.

Glass B will contain water at a temperature of about 80° F.

Container A will cool off fastest.

page 52

The flame appears to be detached from the candle floating in the water because light is refracted, or bent, as it travels from water into glass and from glass into air.

One way to fill a glass with air while it is held underwater is by using a straw. Turn the glass so it is upside down, and hold it just under the surface of the water. Place one end of the straw under the open end of the glass, and blow bubbles underwater so they rise inside the glass. The glass should soon be filled with "breath air." Can you figure out a way to fill the glass with plain "room air"?

If you use a soda straw or medicine dropper to add water very slowly to a glass that is already brimful, you can make the water pile up a little higher than the side of the glass. Can you guess why the water doesn't spill over?

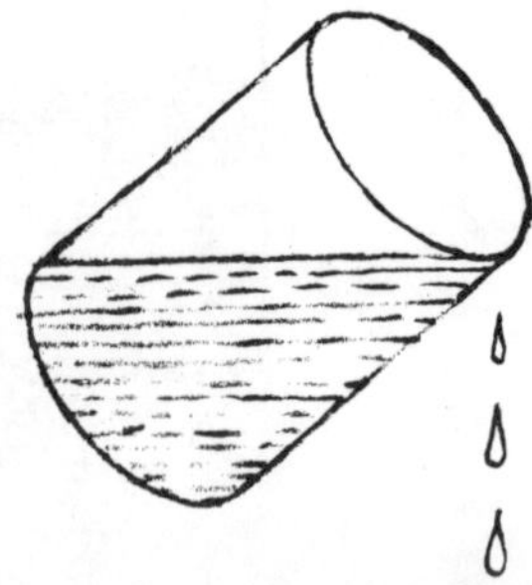

One way to get a can exactly half full of water is to fill the can, then slowly tip it to pour some of the water out. When the water level just reaches the bottom of the can, the can should be just half filled. How can you check to see if it really is?

Muddy water will clear up by itself if allowed to set undisturbed for several days.

Fun with shapes

page 53

Here are three ways the fence can be built. Which way would be cheapest?

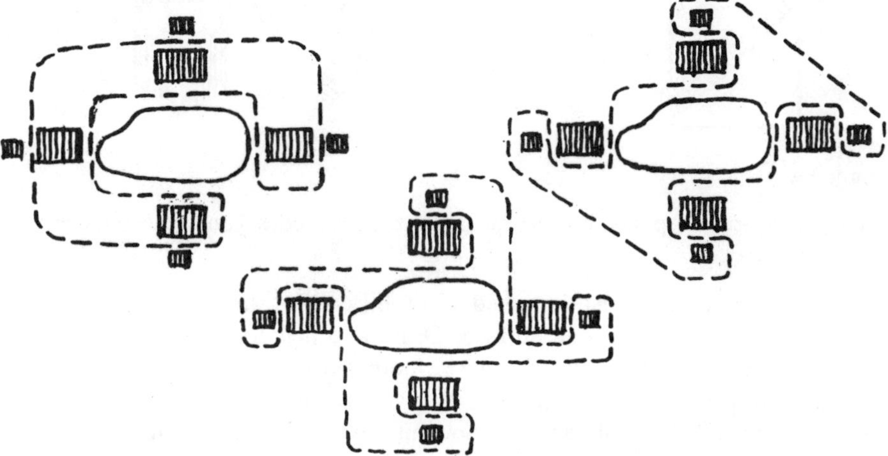

One circle has been divided into eleven parts with four lines. The other circle has been divided into sixteen parts with five lines.

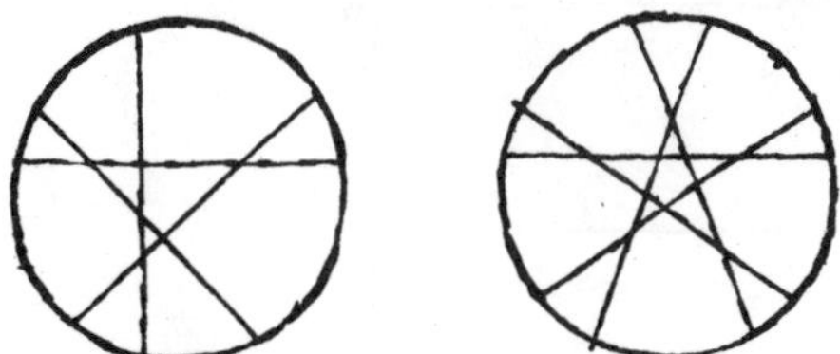

To divide a circle into three equal areas, first draw a diameter and divide it with a ruler into six equal parts as marked by dots, as shown. Then draw semicircles from A to C, E to G, A to E, and C to G, above and below the diameter. Can you divide a circle into four equal areas?

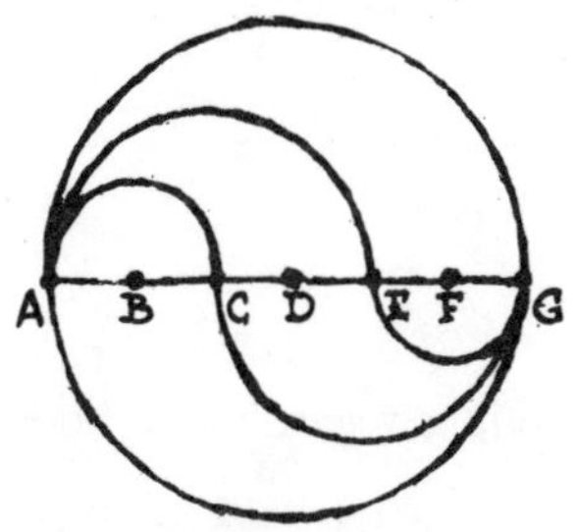

The drawing shows how to cut a cube into three equal pieces.

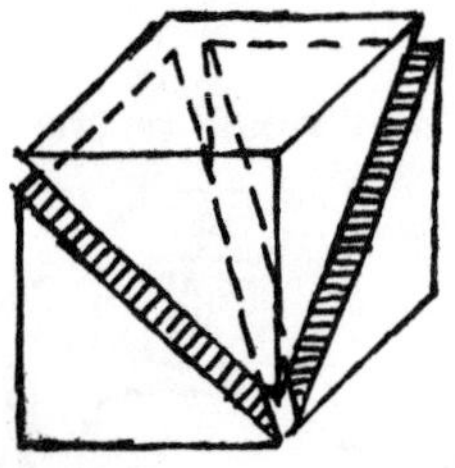

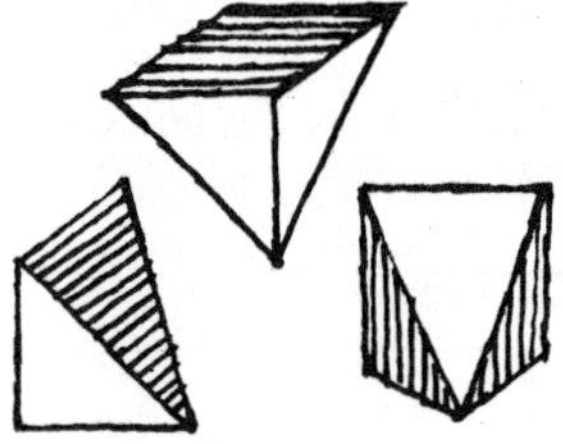

page 54

A square piece of paper has six surfaces, the two sides you write on, and the four edges.

A loop with a half twist is called a Mobius strip. It has the strange property of having only one surface. Draw a pencil line along the loop and you will find that you can mark "both sides" of the strip without lifting your pencil. When a Mobius strip is cut in half, only one larger loop is formed. What will happen if you cut the larger loop in half again?

Shape C is like the piece of paper used to make a cone-shaped paper cup. The drawing shows the shape of an unrolled cardboard tube.

page 55

The mystery photo is a picture of a cabbage that has been cut in half.

Here is how an onion looks when cut in half through its top and bottom.

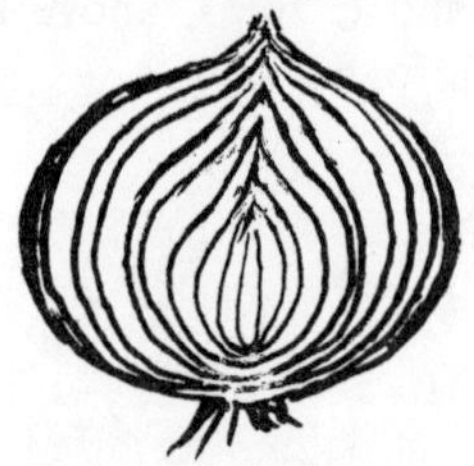

There are no fruits that have the same cross-sections regardless of how they are cut in half.

page 56

Here is how to trace the design.

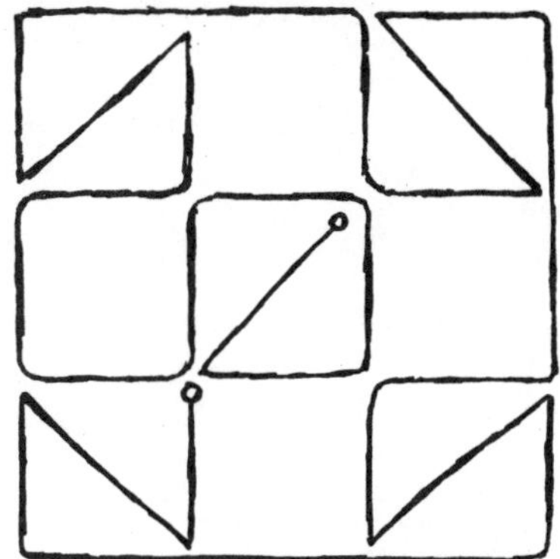

Six pig pens can be made with twelve fence sections in this way.

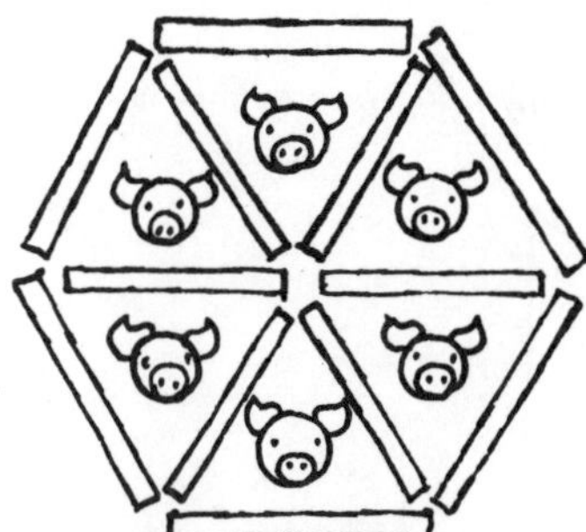

page 57

Here is how you can arrange eight sugar cubes so that each one is at the end of a line of three. Can you find other ways?

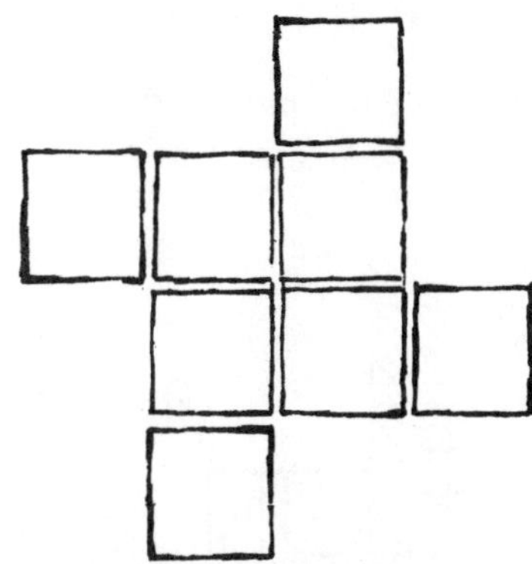

There are thirteen squares in the figure.

Here is a way to make three squares by taking away eight toothpicks.

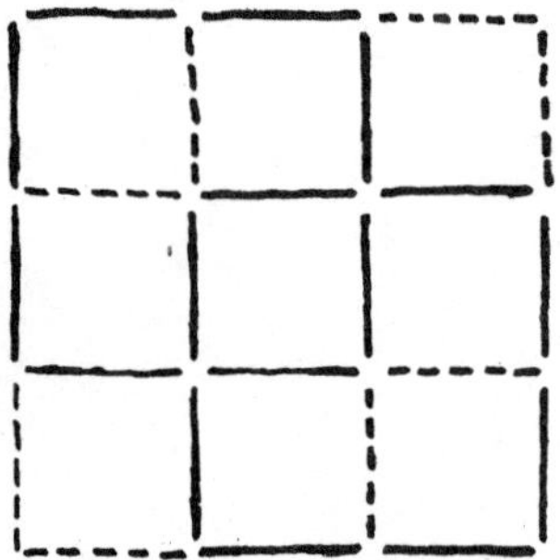

The figure has twenty-eight lines. One way to count them is to redraw the figure.

page 58

The four shapes have been arranged to form a "T."

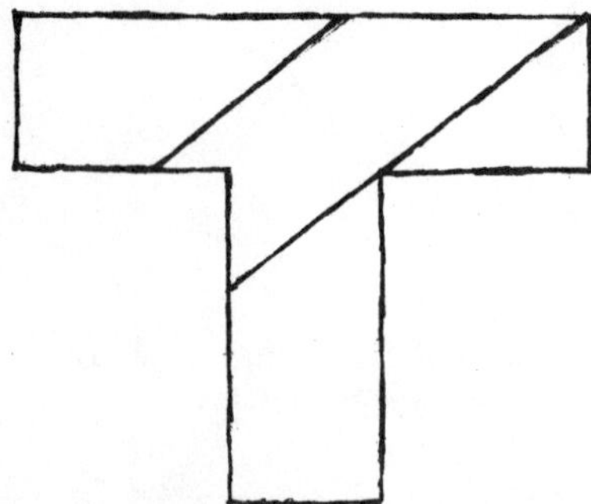

Here is how to divide the design into four equal parts of the same shape.

page 59

This symbol should be in the empty space.

If Ring 3 is cut, all the other rings will come apart. Can you intertwine five loops of string so that they will all come apart when the special one is cut?

page 62

These are three ways the cross can be cut to make a square.

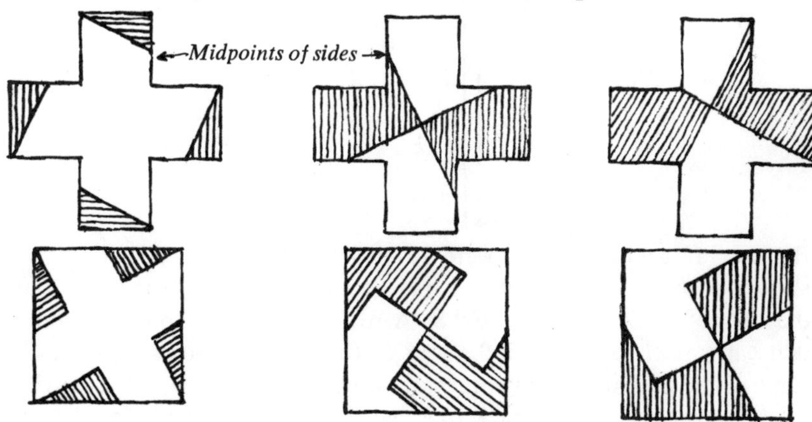

Here is how the paper was folded and punched.

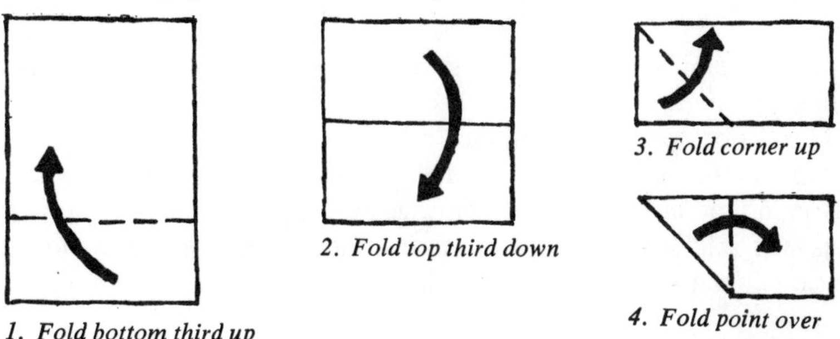

Why is it made this way?

page 63

Top: Balls are made from separate pieces of material that are sewn or glued together to form a sphere. The sketch shows how the pieces of rubber are shaped that were used to make the basketball in the photo.

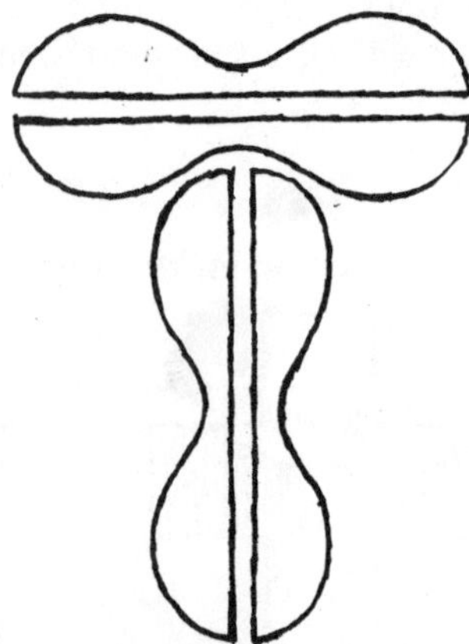

Bottom: If a smooth ball were to travel through the air, it would be slowed down by the zone of high pressure that forms in front of it and by the zone of low pressure behind it. A real golf ball has some 336 dimples that carry pockets of air to the rear of the ball as it spins in flight. Thus some of the air from the high pressure area in front of the ball is carried to the low pressure zone in back to equalize the air pressure. This helps the ball to travel farther.

page 64

Top: The spiral seam of a soda straw strengthens the straw to prevent it from bending, especially when it becomes wet.
Middle: Round pencils roll off the desk easier than hexagonal pencils.
Bottom: Silver coins were originally knurled to prevent people from shaving a little metal from the coin's edge. The silver removed from many coins was sold for a nice profit. Coins with knurled edges could not be shaved without being easily detected.

page 65

Top: Square milk bottles take up less space in the milk truck containers and in the refrigerator than round bottles.

Bottom: The sketch shows how the plastic bottles can be packed with very little lost space. A square-sided plastic bottle would have to be made from thicker plastic to prevent the sides from bulging out.

page 66

Top: The zigzag roof provides the support necessary to hold itself up. A flat roof would require heavy beams.
Bottom: The beams sticking out of the wall are extensions of the roof rafters. They are known as "flying buttresses," and prevent the weight of the roof from pushing out the wall at the top.

page 67

Top: The spaces were left in the bridge railing to allow for expansion when the temperature of the steel rises on warm days. If the railing were made without spaces, it would buckle on hot days.

On certain surfaces such as ice or a wet road a tire with tread does increase friction between the rubber and the road. However, on dry pavement, friction is increased by a smooth tire since more rubber is in contact with the road.

page 68

Top: High towers reduce the strain on the main cables that support the roadway of the bridge.
Bottom: The large tank is an old rain barrel, once used to collect rain water from the roof in times before electric water pumps were invented.

Noise

page 69

Shortening the air column of the hose trombone will raise the pitch of the sound.

The soda straw will make higher notes as it is cut shorter and shorter.

page 70

When blown into, the bottle with more water gives a higher sound than the emptier bottle. The reverse will occur when the bottles are tapped with a pencil.

page 71

To hear a watch tick at the distance of three feet, hold one end of a yardstick against the watch. Then press the other end of the stick against the bone behind your ear.

Probably the hardest combination of fingers to move together is your middle finger and little finger. Much practice and exercise are necessary to move all the fingers easily in different combinations.

page 72

Astonauts on the moon communicate with one another by radio.

The pitch of a piano string is determined by its thickness as well as its length. The longer strings in large pianos are thinner than the corresponding strings in small pianos. Tightening and loosening a string also changes its pitch. Does tightening make a string sound higher or lower?

The noise from a popping balloon is made by the air rushing out.

The noise in ginger ale is caused by the carbon dioxide bubbles that break as they float to the surface.

An empty glass picks up other sound waves already in the air and directs them into your ear.

For science experts only

page 73

Man is the mammal that has the longest life span.

The seeds of a strawberry are on the outside. What fruits have only one seed?

When a goldfish is out of water, its gill filaments clump together like wet feathers. This makes their surface too small to absorb enough oxygen from the air. The gill filaments are spread apart in the water.

Soil is slowly formed from rocks on mountain tops, but it is quickly washed away by water to less steep areas where it accumulates.

Use a globe to find out what is underneath you.

page 74

Wheel B turns in the same direction as Gear A.

Gear B is turning around three times a minute, which is the same speed as Gear A. Two gears with an equal number of teeth will turn at the same speed regardless of the number and size of gears between them.

page 75

When shaken, much of the dissolved CO_2 gas becomes less attached in the liquid. Opening the bottle suddenly releases the pressure. Then the gas rushes out of the top, carrying much of the soda with it.

A tin can is made from steel that is coated with a thin layer of tin. When the tin wears off, the steel underneath rusts. Can you figure out why cans are not made of solid tin so they would never rust?

The weight of a tank will become heavier as helium gas is pumped into it.

Even though helium is lighter than air, it still weighs something. If this is so, why does a balloon filled with helium float?

A mirror can be no smaller than one half of your height for you to be able to see yourself from head to toe.

page 76

When seen from the earth, the earth looks larger than any other planet.

The only planet that we can be sure has canals, icecaps, and an atmosphere is the earth.

The first satellite to circle the earth was the moon. Can the moon ever be seen during the daytime?

During the days when the sky is clear, you can see the sun, which is just a close star.

When the moon is full, there would be a "new earth" seen from the moon. How would the earth look when there is a new moon?

During the day, the air that has been warmed up by the sun rises and pushes aside the cooler air. By sunset, there are many moving masses of air at different temperatures between your eyes and the sun. The warmer and cooler masses of air bend the light in different ways, often making the sun appear to be oval, or sometimes other shapes. At dawn, the sunlight reaches your eyes through cool air that bends all the light rays in about the same way, so the sun's round shape does not usually appear changed.

page 77

The sun's heat is created by an atomic reaction as hydrogen is changed into helium. The sun changes matter into energy so fast that its weight is decreasing faster than four million tons a second. But don't worry about the sun burning itself out. It is so big that it should continue to give off light and heat for at least thirty-five billion years.

The spinning earth does not create a wind because the atmosphere spins along with the earth. If a stone is thrown up into the air, it, too, moves along with the earth. Things don't fly off into space because the centrifugal force created by the earth's rotation is not as strong as the earth's gravity.

The propeller blade must spin clockwise when viewed from the front.

page 78

The towers that hold up the Verrazano Bridge each stick "straight up" from the earth. Since the earth is round, and the towers are so far apart, this means that they are not exactly parallel to each other. So they are farther and farther apart as they rise above the water.

The round weights at the ends of their arms were supposed to turn the wheel of the perpetual motion machine. As the wheel turned, the weights at the center of the machine would fall to the ends of their arms, providing leverage to keep the process going. The machine did not work because there were never enough weights at the left-hand rim of the wheel to turn it.

page 79

To make it impossible to kill him, the man said, "I shall be hanged." This meant that he could not have been shot, since then what he said would have been false and he would have to be hanged. If he were hanged, however, what he said would have been a true statement, so he should have been shot.

What we caught we threw away; what we could not catch we kept: bugs in our hair.

The smart prince suggested that the race be run by having each man ride the other man's horse.

page 80

It takes the earth a long time to heat up. Even though the sun is a little farther away from the earth in July and August, the weather is warmer because the earth has had more time to get warm.

The air in most deserts is hot in the daytime because air is warmed by contact with the ground, which soaks up heat from the sun's rays. More of these heat rays reach the ground through the clean, dry air of a desert than through the moist, dusty, and sometimes cloudy air over a wooded or grassy region.

The ground just beneath the surface is usually cooler than the air above. Once past a certain depth, though, the temperature begins to increase.

The cooling system of a refrigerator takes heat from the inside of the refrigerator and releases it into the room. If the refrigerator door were left open, there could be no change in temperature.

Photographs can be held either way.

A pointed nail acts as a wedge and may split the wood apart. A blunt nail often punches out a little wood as it is hammered through the board.

Kitchen chemistry

page 83

Just before the match lowered into CO_2 goes out, the flame burns a short distance above the stick.

The tablet dissolves faster when it has been broken into pieces. Hot water also makes a tablet dissolve more quickly.

page 84

More than 90 per cent of lettuce is water.

page 85

You can dissolve more than ten teaspoons of salt in a glass of water if the water is hot.
One way to separate the pepper from the salt is to dump the mixture into a glass of water. The salt will dissolve, while the pepper floats on top. Another way is to use static electricity. Run a comb through your hair several times, and then hold it close to the mixture. The pepper should fly up and stick to the comb.

The best way to find out which cup has the baking soda is to add some vinegar to both cups. Vinegar makes soda give off CO_2 gas, which will form bubbles.

To make a glass of water that contains just one eighth of a drop of milk, first use a straw to place one drop of milk into a full glass of water. Stir the mixture, then dump out half and add more water until the glass is filled again. Do this twice more, and you will have one eighth of a drop of milk in the water. How can you make a glass of water that contains one fifth of a drop of milk?

Fun with numbers

page 87

Here are two more ways for arranging the nine digits to equal 100.

$$\begin{array}{r} 56 \\ 8 \\ 4 \\ 3 \\ \hline 71 \\ 29 \\ \hline 100 \end{array} \qquad \begin{array}{r} 95\tfrac{1}{2} \\ 4\tfrac{38}{76} \\ \hline 100 \end{array}$$

The names of the numbers were arranged alphabetically.

$1\frac{1}{6}$ is a number that can be added to 7 or multiplied by 7 to give the same answer.

When 142857 is multiplied by 2, the product is 285714. Notice that the answer contains the same numbers as 142857, and in the same sequence. A similar answer occurs when 142857 is multiplied by 3, 4, 5, and 6. But when it is multiplied by 7, the answer is 999,999. Can you find any order in the answers obtained by multiplying 142857 by larger numbers?

Here is how each number series should be continued:

A. 1 4 7 10 13. Each number is three more than the number before it.

B. 1 2 4 8 16 32. Each number is two times the number before it.

C. 1 3 4 7 11 18 29 47. Each number is the sum of the two numbers before it.

D. 1 2 3 5 7 11 13. The numbers in this series are all *prime numbers*. A prime number is a number that cannot be evenly divided by any number except itself and 1.

page 88

After the milk and orange juice are mixed, the amount of milk in the orange juice is the same as the amount of orange juice in the milk. Can you figure out why?

For all of the eight men to shake hands with each other, there need only be twenty eight handshakes.

A twenty-pound fish weighs ten pounds plus half its weight.

There are six drawers in the chest.

page 89

The cheapest way to make the long chain would be to take apart one section of chain and use the three links to join together the other four sections.

A line of one million nickels would be about thirteen miles long.

To find the weight of one page in a telephone book, divide the weight of the whole book by the number of pages. The book can be weighed on a bathroom scale.

page 90

The minute hand of a clock passes the hour hand only 11 times in 12 hours.

It takes 65 minutes and 27 seconds for the minute and hour hands of a clock to meet again after meeting. Since the hands pass one another 11 times in 12 hours, you can divide the number of seconds in 12 hours by 11 to get the answer.

It will take 11¼ seconds for the clock to strike ten o'clock. Since there are four time intervals in 5 seconds, each interval is 1¼ seconds long.

The electricity was off for 7½ hours, and went back on at 1:00 A.M.

Funny trees

page 91

When the pine was young, a large tree fell on it. The pine was bent in such a way that it grew in a loop as it straightened up.

page 92

Top: The tree was not bent closer to the ground when it was smaller. All upward growth occurs from the top of a tree. What probably happened was that a larger tree or branch fell and pushed aside the growing tip of the smaller tree. The treetop remained bent, and the new growth continued straight up.
Bottom: The top of the tree under the wires was cut away by the power company.

page 93

Top: The lopsided pine tree is near the ocean. Strong winds blowing from the sea prevent the tree from growing normally. Where else might you find such a tree?
Bottom: The tree grew in the unusual shape after it was almost blown down.

page 94

Top: The limb from the tree on the left grew toward the other tree until the limb and tree rubbed together. As the rubbing wore off the bark from a part of each, sticky liquid from the wood helped join them together.
Bottom: Over the years, the soil around the tree has gradually eroded away. Roots that were once underground are left exposed.

page 95

Top: The inside of the tree was almost completely eaten away by ants.
Bottom: The wires through the tree trunk were nailed to it a long time ago for a fence. Then, as the tree grew larger, it grew over the wires. Do the fence wires also get carried higher above the ground as the tree gets bigger?

page 96

Top: The tree seed was blown into a crack between the chimney bricks. It

sprouted and continued to grow, using minerals from the mortar and rain water.
Bottom: The seeds became buried in the ground before the blacktop paving was laid. The seedlings later germinated and forced their way through the asphalt.

page 97

The tree grew faster during its older years. Notice how the rings became larger.

page 98

Top: The off-center rings came from a tree that was tipped over by a windstorm when it was very young.
Bottom: The piece of wood lettered "B" was cut closest to the center of the log. The rings on this piece are more curved.

Bulbs and batteries

page 99

Top: The filament in the bulb is a better conductor of electricity than faucet water is, so most of the current flows through the bulb.
Bottom: A light bulb is almost empty inside except for a little argon gas and nitrogen gas. When a hole is made in a bulb underwater, the water will fill up most of the empty space. The little bubble left is the argon and nitrogen gas..

page 100

The diagram shows how a circuit can be arranged to make the bell ring when either switch is closed.

In this circuit, one switch lights the bulb while the other switch rings the bell.

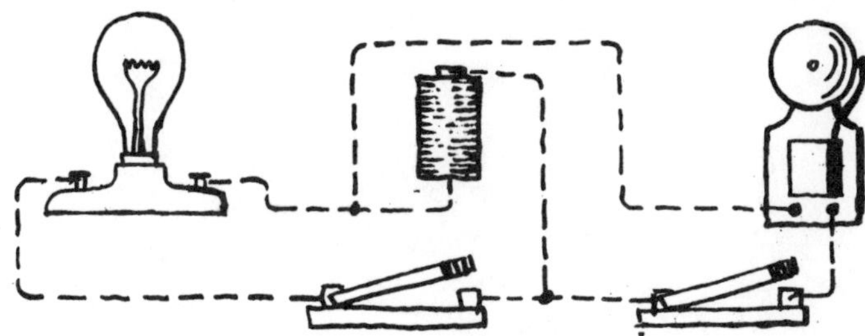

When the switch is closed in the complicated circuit, the bell will *stop* ringing. Will the light bulb light?

page 101

The battery connected to the two bulbs in series will last longest. Bulbs A and B will be brightest. Which battery will last longest?

page 102

When the penny lands between the two aluminum foil strips, the circuit is completed.

page 103

An aspirin tablet or even a grain of salt could be substituted for the sugar cube in the rain alarm clothespin switch.

page 104

Top: The photo was taken looking straight down into a porcelain light socket.
Bottom: This picture shows the lighted filament of a clear bulb.

What will happen if?

page 105

Bottle D will collect the smallest amount of rain water, while Bottle B will fill up first. Which bottle will make the best rain gauge?

A cold ball does not bounce as high as a ball at room temperature. If the ball is heated in a warm (but not lighted) oven, will it bounce even higher than it does at room temperature?

As the candle burns, the wax from the lower end will melt faster. Soon the candle will be balanced straight across. Then it will wobble back and forth like a little seesaw. After a while, it may balance again.

page 106

Although carbon dioxide is heavier than air, the weight of the materials inside the bag is unchanged. Since the plastic glove takes up more space, however, it is buoyed up by the air, making the scale go up on the left side.

The weight of the sealed jar and food will not change as the food decays and becomes moldy. What would happen if the jar is left uncovered?

page 107

The weight of popcorn becomes less after popping. When heated, the moisture inside the kernel turns to steam and causes the corn to explode. Thus, the popped corn is lighter because of its water loss.

When the straw is moved up higher on the strings, it takes a longer time for the motion of one pendulum to be transferred to the other pendulum. What will happen if the straw is tipped so it is higher on one string? Connect the two pendulums with a piece of string instead of a straw. Now what happens?

page 108

The two equal weights will continue moving for a long time, depending upon how heavy they are and the length of the strings.

The smaller weight swings in a circle around the string of the heavier weight while the heavier weight moves slowly back and forth like a pendulum.

page 109

Here is where the strips will probably rip when pulled:

A. At one end next to where you hold it.
B. At the narrow end by your fingers.
C. At the crease.
D. Above the narrow notch.
E. Above the sharp notch.
F. Above the hole by the edge.
G. At the hole closer to the edge.

page 110

The wax drop at End B of each aluminum strip should melt first. Would a wax drop on a strip of aluminum foil ever melt if it were a foot away from the place being heated?

Experiments on you

page 111

To break a toothpick held between three fingers, slap your hand down on a desk or table.

It is almost impossible to break an egg if you squeeze it the long way between your hands.

If you are strong, you can pick up a chair by lifting at the bottom of one leg with just one hand. Grip one of the back legs and lift the other three legs a little off the floor. Then quickly lift the chair, keeping the leg you are holding lower than the other legs.

page 113

You can touch your left elbow with your right hand but not your left hand.

It is not possible to catch a baseball while keeping your hands perfectly still.

Only a left-handed person can write the number 6 while moving his left leg in a clockwise motion. If you are right-handed, see if you can do it when moving your *right* leg.

It is impossible to inhale through your nose at the same time you exhale through your mouth.

You will probably have trouble chewing your food by moving your jaw only up and down. Why does a cow chew its cud by moving its jaw back and forth?

It is almost impossible to swallow when the tongue is blocked with a spoon. Food in the mouth is normally squeezed backward by the tongue pressing against the roof of the mouth.

It is possible to swallow water while you are upside down. Muscles in your throat contract and force the water up into your stomach. Why must birds lift their heads in order to swallow?

page 115

It is impossible to see anything in complete darkness.

A sound made at your right reaches your right ear slightly before your left ear. This is how you are able to tell in which direction a noise is coming

from. If your ears were close together on your face, you would have much more trouble in telling where a sound was made. Could you see better if your eyes were located where your ears are?
If your ears were where your eyes are, you would not be able to hear as well.

page 116

Not all parts of the body are sensitive to hot and cold in the same way. Water of the same temperature can feel cool to your hand and warm inside your mouth.

Fluid from the blood continually seeps through the walls of the blood vessels. This excess liquid is picked up by the lymph system and returned to the heart in the lymph tubes. Movement of the arm and leg muscles forces the liquid to move through the tubes. At night, when most muscles are not being used, the lymph system cannot remove all the excess liquid. This causes your body to swell up a little bit during the night.

Blood in a vein is blue because it does not contain much oxygen. When you bleed from a vein, the oxygen in the air immediately mixes with the blue blood and changes its color to red.

More blood collects in the lower hand and makes it redder.

The carbon dioxide gas in soda causes it to be slightly acidic. The delicate lining of the food tube can become irritated by large quantities of even weak carbonic acid.

page 118

Your hair grows about one inch a month. You can get some idea of your hair's growth rate by noticing how long it gets between haircuts.

David Webster is a former elementary and junior high school science teacher and served for four years as director of science for the Lincoln, Massachusetts, school system. He is now a science consultant for the Wellesley public schools, and has written numerous science-activity articles for children's magazines. In addition, he works as a carpenter and housebuilder.

A man of boundless energy and imagination, Mr. Webster is co-owner and co-director of Camp Netop, a boys' camp in Maine, and he has been a Boy Scout leader for many years. Mr. Webster and his family live in Lincoln, Massachusetts.